THE HIPPIE HANDBOOK

BY CHELSEA CAIN
ILLUSTRATIONS BY LIA MITERNIQUE

CHRONICLE BOOKS
San Francisco

ACKNOWLEDGMENTS

Special thanks to Diana Abu-Jaber, Karen Karbo, Whitney Otto, and Cynthia Whitcomb, all writers of great wit and generosity. You inspire me endlessly. Thanks also to Fred and Laura, Steve Mockus, Lia Miternique, the Noodge, the Pod, and to my dad, Larry Schmidt, whose knowledge of the minutiae of composting continues to slay me.

- -

Library of Congress Cataloging-in-Publication Data:
Cain, Chelsea.
   The hippie handbook : how to tie-dye a T-shirt, flash a peace sign, and other essential skills for the carefree life / Chelsea Cain ; illustrations by Lia Miternique.
      p. cm.
   ISBN 0-8118-4320-3
   1. Hippies—Life skills guides. 2. Counterculture—Handbooks, manuals, etc. I. Title.
   HQ799.5C325 2004
   305.5'68—dc22

                          2003027897

 Manufactured in Canada
Printed on recycled paper

Designed by Tom & John: A Design Collaborative

Distributed in Canada by Raincoast Books
9050 Shaughnessy Street
Vancouver, British Columbia V6P 6E5

10 9 8 7 6 5 4 3 2

Chronicle Books LLC
85 Second Street
San Francisco, California 94105
www.chroniclebooks.com

for Marc Mohan
and every kid named "Sunshine"

TABLE OF
CONTENTS

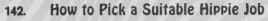

INTRODUCTION

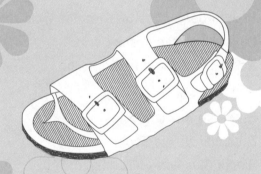

I spent my early childhood in a hippie commune in Iowa, and I guess one way or another I have been trying to get back ever since. As the child of hippies, I can say with the utmost confidence that there is no better counterculture in which to grow up. The craft projects alone would keep most kids stimulated for the better part of a decade. How many toddlers today know how to macramé a sweater for a goat?

We lived in an old, white farmhouse with several outbuildings that served as shelter for various dogs, horses, sheep, goats, and chickens, and whoever couldn't fit in the house. My dad had decided not to go fight in Vietnam, and so he and my mother were living "underground." (For many years, in the later part of my childhood, I thought that when I was a baby we had all lived in subterranean tunnels.) They had spent some time traveling in Europe, become homesick, and returned to the States. As Midwesterners are by nature taciturn, Iowa seemed as good a place as any to hide out. They moved into the farmhouse and pretty soon friends started to drop by. Months passed. The friends never left.

There wasn't a lot of money. We ate what we grew in the garden and served millet casserole because it was cheap and fed plenty. For years we didn't have a telephone, or a TV, or flushing toilets. But we played music on the porch for fun and I got to wear whatever I wanted and run free in the cornfields and help the adults plan The Dream at night.

My parents were back-to-the-landers. My dad, in his eventual trial for draft resistance, stated his profession as "subsistence farmer." My parents and their friends believed in living outside the war machine, off the grid, out of the box. We made candles and clothes and hanging plant holders, not because these things weren't available else-where but because not buying stuff was a radical act of social resistance.

This do-it-yourself approach was a defining aspect of the hippie trip. Between 1965 and 1975, hippies figured out how to do a lot of stuff. This book is a collection of some of it. These are not just timeless skills; they are the tools of a movement, as useful today as they were pre-Watergate. How many neo-hippies have gone to a Phish show only to embarrass themselves with their poorly executed tie-dyed apparel? How many young-hippies-turned-old-hippies no longer remember the nuances of composting?

Suffice it to say, this is the book I wish I had had growing up. Being a hippie is not easy, and comprehensive resource guides are few. The movement has changed. Yet hippies have persevered, and the skill set has remained remarkably consistent. Maybe if more of us had access to the movement's means, we might better protect its ethos. (I imagine a world in which *all* people have the ability to make sand candles.) In any case, I hope that this small guide will promote understanding, as well as an increase in May Day parties. After all, hippies are the dolphins of our species: playful, resilient, social, fetishized by some, dismissed by others. They represent all that is optimistic and outrageous and youthful in each of us. Plus, they have the best hair.

If you are a hippie, I hope that you find this book handy. If you are not a hippie, beware. Once you know the joy of a good barefoot amble, it's a short road to selling homemade beads off a batik blanket in Berkeley.

See you there.

Chelsea Cain
Portland, Oregon

HOW TO WEAR
Your Hair
LIKE A HIPPIE

THE BASICS

* Shampoo as rarely as possible.

* Cut your hair as rarely as possible.

* If you have to cut your hair, cut it yourself or have someone—preferably a roommate or hitchhiker—cut it for you.

* Braiding is OK.

* NEVER shave legs or underarms.

* NEVER bikini wax.

HAIR ACCESSORIES

* Kerchiefs (especially rolled and tied around forehead)

* Native American braid ties

* Tooled leather barrettes

* Beads

* Rubber bands

* Roach clips

RECIPE FOR NATURAL BLOND HIGHLIGHTS

1. Squeeze fresh lemon juice into a bowl. (One nice-size lemon should do it.)

2. Add one teaspoon of salt and stir.

3. Work into hair.

4. Expose hair to midday sun for at least two hours. (Attend outdoor Phish concert, Rainbow Gathering, or other peaceful event.)

5. Rinse and air dry.

RECOMMENDED PRODUCTS

* **Dr. Bronner's Peppermint Pure-Castile Soap (also good for shaving, shampooing, massage, teeth cleaning, and bathing)**

* **Eucalyptus oil (A small amount rubbed into the scalp has an invigorating, aromatherapeutic effect. Too much will make hair look oily—which, of course, may be the look you're going for.)**

Observing a trend in folk circles involving barrettes with long strips of leather and feathers dangling from them, I wandered at age eight into a small, sweet-smelling store in Key West, Florida, to purchase a similar contraption. Mine was even better. The leather strips and feathers were not simply attached to a barrette but could instead be affixed to any sort of barrette with a handy silver clamp. Later I would learn that I had purchased a roach clip, but by then I had already worn it in my hair for most of third grade.

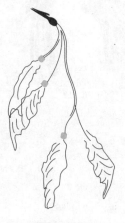

ROACH CLIP

BARRETTE

HAIR ARCHETYPES: MALE

JOHN LENNON

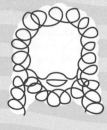

CAT STEVENS

**JIMI HENDRIX /
ART GARFUNKEL**

MY DAD

BOB MARLEY

FACIAL HAIR ARCHETYPES: MALE

MOUSTACHE:
DAVID CROSBY

SIDEBURNS:
NEIL YOUNG

BEARD:
JERRY GARCIA

HAIR ARCHETYPES: FEMALE

BOB MARLEY

JOAN BAEZ

HOW TO
Dress
LIKE A HIPPIE

Anything goes.

POSSIBILITIES

* **Go naked (but wear sunscreen).**
* **Wear a costume:**

Jesus. Biblical chic is easy and always in style: tunic, robe or caftan, sandals.

Oh, pioneer! Think *Little House on the Prairie:* Long skirts and bonnets for women; breeches, work boots, and suspenders for men. This is the back-to-the-land gold standard. You should look like you have just raised a barn and are ready for a hootenanny.

Rock-star bohemian. Marianne Faithfull. Recently deposed Eastern European princess. Anything trimmed with alpaca. Tons of bracelets. Long-sleeved leotards.

Counterculture casual. Old blue jeans, preferably torn and/or patched. East Indian–style shirts or skirts that you have made yourself from a pattern of your own creation. Leather vest and bare skin. Bare feet or, possibly, clogs.

Mix-and-match. Edwardian top hats, boas, thrift-store evening gowns. Mix patterns, colors, fabrics, and eras.

(continued)

JESUS

OH, PIONEER!

ROCK-STAR BOHEMIAN

COUNTERCULTURE CASUAL

MIX-AND-MATCH

At any given time I had more than a dozen leotards (which is a lot of any one thing for a hippie to have), in every color you can imagine. I spent a lot of time as a kid trying to figure out how to pee without taking off my leotard. I had heard women talking about this. I knew it could be done. Some had snaps in the crotch, which made peeing easier, but most did not. Peeing while wearing the snapless kind required pulling the leotard crotch to the side with one hand in order to avoid getting it wet. I was in my mid-twenties before I mastered the art of urinating fully clothed.

CLASSIC ITEMS FOR EVERY HIPPIE'S WARDROBE

For men

* Arizona Birkenstocks

* Old blue jeans with an American flag patch or peace dove on rear pocket

* Work shirt

* Surplus Navy pants

* Any item of clothing that fastens with leather laces

For women

* Calfskin lace-up boots with fringe (regrettably dubbed "squaw boots")

* Moroccan caftan in basic blue

* Leotard (long-sleeved, black), worn braless

* Ankle-length East Indian skirt

* Fringed, embroidered shawl

Hippie accessories

* Face paint (rainbows, unicorns, etc.)

* Armpit/leg hair

* Silver bracelets (at least a hundred, worn all at once)

* Mexican jewelry of any kind

* Indian jewelry of any kind

* Native American jewelry of any kind

* Favorite gems (amber, turquoise, or cat's eye)

* Anklets that jingle

* Hats (floppy, vintage, wizard hats, Cat-in-the-Hat hats)

* Granny glasses

* Statement buttons ("Take a Hippie to Lunch," "Immoral Minority," "Impeach Nixon," "Ban the Bomb," or "Ban the Bra")

* Leather belts

* Purses (ethnic woven, hemp, or hand-tooled leather)

* Anything beaded

* No watch

HOW TO
Tell Time
LIKE A HIPPIE

1. Look at the position of the sun.

2. When the sun is directly overhead it is noon. That means that if the sun is somewhere between the eastern horizon and directly overhead, it is sometime between sunrise and noon.

3. If the sun is somewhere between directly overhead and the western horizon, it is sometime between noon and sunset.

4. If you can determine the exact time of sunrise and sunset (through your local newspaper), you will be able to more accurately gauge the time as indicated by the position of the sun.

5. On overcast days, ask everyone you pass what time it is.

6. Don't worry about the time—it's the day of the week that's important.

7. Don't worry about the day of the week—it's the month that's important.

Hippies enjoy a casual relationship with time. Most hippies do not like to wear watches, since watches imply that one has to be somewhere or do something at a particular time, and this goes against hippie mores. This can present a problem for children, who occasionally require being picked up from, or delivered to, some sort of organized activity. My mother and I once went three days before we realized that daylight savings time had kicked in. I have compensated for the lack of time consciousness in my upbringing by developing a neurotic impulse toward punctuality. When I arrive for an appointment (dinner at your house, for example), I am not on time—I am thirty minutes early. Even if it means sitting in the car out front for a half hour before I come to your door.

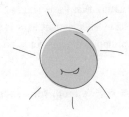

NOON

BETWEEN NOON AND SUNSET

25

HOW TO
Anthropomorphize
INANIMATE OBJECTS

Perhaps it is the hippie's spiritual nature that leads him or her to enthusiastically imagine that all inanimate objects have feelings. Is it hard to believe that a bulletin board can have a soul? If you are a hippie, the answer is no.

ANTHROPOMORPHIZING TIPS

* Name the inanimate object—a coffee mug, for example.

* Talk to the coffee mug.

* Consider the feelings of the coffee mug. How does it feel in its situation? (How would you feel in its place?) Is it rarely used? Does it have a chip?

* Does it long to be around other coffee mugs? Is it jealous of the teacups?

* Take action to make the coffee mug happy.

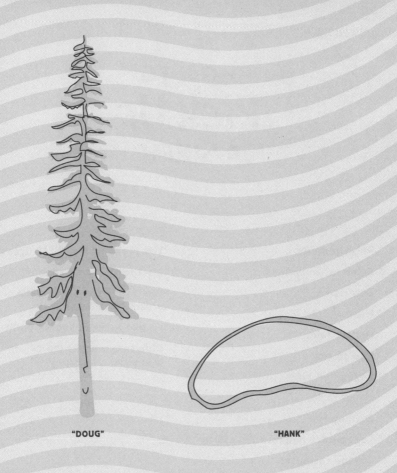

"DOUG"

"HANK"

When I was a kid, I named everything around me: my bed, all my necklaces, the Doug firs by the bus stop, the Holly bush in our side yard. I once had a deflated bicycle tire that I had found on the road in Key West, and I cared for it all summer. His name was Hank. Although I have mostly weaned myself of this habit as an adult, my boyfriend and I had a window we called William until quite recently. William was replaced by a prettier window and taken away on a neighborhood clean-up day. It was very sad.

HOW TO
Pick Up
A HIPPIE

WHERE TO MEET A HIPPIE

* Phish concerts
* Rainbow Gatherings
* Dog parks
* Head shops
* Pottery fairs
* Kite stores
* Vegetarian cafés
* Hemp rallies
* Burning Man
* Cooperative natural food stores
* College campuses
* Fair-trade craft stores
* Protests
* Banjo lessons
* Belly-dancing classes
* Renaissance fairs
* Reggae festivals

ICEBREAKERS

* "You look just like Ali McGraw!"
* "Want to sign my petition?"
* "Can I offer you a non-GMO, organic meatless patty?"
* "I'd like to make you an outfit."
* "Didn't we meet at the psychedelic symposium?"

HOW TO
Name Your
HIPPIE BABY

* Wait until you're introduced.

* Think noun: August Autumn Bear Rainbow River Summer Trout Tuesday Winter

* Think weather: Breeze Hail Rain Storm Sun Sunny Sunshine Wind

* Think horticulture: Basil Begonia Blossom Clover Daisy Earth Fern Flower Heather Iris Jasmine Lavender Leaf Magnolia Marigold Meadow Moss Petal Rose Saffron Sage Seed Sunflower Thyme Violet Willow

* Think fantasy: Avalon Bilbo Dragon Frodo Galadriel Grimm Merlin Morgan Pegasus Puck Ranger Rogue Tolkien

* Think place: Asia Carmel Chelsea China Dakota Desert Fillmore Georgia India Ocean Tibet Zion

* Think Carlos Castaneda: Aurora Bud Cassiopia Cloud Cosmic Eclipse Haley Leary Light Rainbow Sky Skye Skylar Skyler Soul Spirit Star Starbright Stardust Starlight Starr Starshine

* Change C to K: Amerika Elektra Krystal

When in doubt give your baby the last name of someone who played in the Monterey Pop Festival (e.g., Crosby, Hendrix, Joplin, Redding, or Shankar).

My parents waited until I was six weeks old to name me. They were actually waiting until I "named myself," and it seems I must have taken a while to decide. My grandmother, who was finding it difficult to explain to her friends that her granddaughter did not yet have a name, kept asking my parents how long they were going to let this go on. "How can we name her?" my father asked. "We don't even know her." Finally, one day my mother was nursing me while listening to Judy Collins sing "Chelsea Morning" and I gurgled. They called me Chelsea Snow: "Chelsea" because I liked the song, and "Snow" because I was born during a blizzard.

OTHER POSSIBILITIES

A

Alice
Allegra
Alma
Amethyst
Andromeda
Angel
Ariel
Athena
Augie
Avery
Azura

B

Blaze
Bliss
Blue
Bohdim
Brianna
Burgundy
Butterfly
Buzz

C

Cady
Carmen
Casey
Cassidy
Celeste
Chakra
Charity
Che
Cherish
Chloe
Coral
Coriander
Coyote
Crimson
Crystal
Cyress

D

Dancer
Dawn
Deja
Destiny
Dharma
Doobie
Dude
Dusk
Dylan

E

Echo
Electra
Ember
Emerald
Ethan
Evan

F

Faith
Feather
Felicity
Flow
Floyd
Free
Freedom

G

Gaia
Garcia
Gia
Grace

H

Hailey
Hanna
Hannah
Harmony
Heady
Heart
Holly
Honesty
Honey
Hope

J

Jade
Janis
Jay
Jerry
Jewel
Joplin
Journey
Joy
Julia
Justice

K

Karma
Kaya
Kelsey

L

Lennon
Liberty
Lilly
Logan
Lolita
Love
Luna
Lylee
Lyric

M

Madrah
Mandy
Manu
Marley
Maya
Melody
Micha
Mirakel
Mist
Moon
Moonshine
Morning

N

Nico

O

Om
Opal
Orion

P

Paisley
Papers
Patches
Patchouli
Peace
Peaceful
Phoebe
Pink
Promise
Prosperity
Prudence

Q

Quentin
Quincy
Quinn

R

Rana
Rayne
Rayon
Renee
Revelation
Revolution
Rex
River
Rufus

S

Sadie
Sapphire
Sativa
Scarlett
Sebastian
Secret
Serena
Serenity
Shadow
Shannon
Shalom
Shanti
Stone
Sugar

Sunburst
Sunstar

T

Talia
Terra
Timothy
Topaz
Trent
Trey
Trinity
Tuesday

V

Vishnu

W

Welcome

X

Xavier

Z

Zachary
Zen
Ziggy
Zoe
Zooey
Zora

NOTE: THIS BELT IS PURELY DECORATIVE AND WILL NOT HOLD UP PANTS.

HOW TO
Macramé

Macramé is a popular hippie craft because it is very versatile and frankly pretty easy. Once you master the basics of macramé, it won't be long before you are a macramé maniac. (Note: People do not really like to receive macramé as a gift.)

WHAT TO MACRAMÉ

* Pot holders
* Plant hangers
* Vests
* Shawls
* Wallet chains
* Sunglass bands
* Guitar straps
* Purses

WHAT YOU NEED

* Two 5-foot pieces of yarn (they can be the same or different colors)

* A wooden or plastic ring (about 1 inch in diameter)— this will be your anchor

----

When my mother was nineteen her favorite outfit was a yellow macramé minidress. Whenever she wore it out to a party, she noticed that all the boys asked her to dance. Eventually she realized that, under the black lights, her macramé dress disappeared entirely and all that remained of her were the whites of her eyes, her teeth, and her bright white bra and underpants.

(continued)

HOW TO MAKE A BELT USING THE BASIC SQUARE KNOT

1. Fold one piece of yarn exactly in half, so that the loose ends match up.

2. Holding the yarn by the loop end, pull the loop through the ring 1 inch. The loop is now on one side of the ring, while the rest of the yarn is on the other.

3. Holding the two ends together, guide them under the ring and through the loop. Pull tight to form a knot around the base of the loop.

4. Repeat with the other piece of yarn, so that you have two knotted pieces of yarn next to each other at the base of the ring.

5. The four loose ends of yarn will now be hanging side by side under the knots. Imagine that each is numbered, from the left, 1, 2, 3, and 4.

6. Thread yarn 1 over yarns 2 and 3, and under yarn 4.

7. Thread yarn 4 under yarns 3 and 2 and over yarn 1, through the loop you have created between yarns 1 and 2 in step 6.

8. Thread yarn 1 over yarns 3 and 2.

9. Thread yarn 4 over yarn 1 (now on the left), under yarns 2 and 3 and over yarn 1 again (now on the right) through the loop you created between yarn 1 and 3 in step 8.

10. You've made a square knot. Pull it tight.

11. Repeat steps 6 through 10 until your row of square knots is the length of the circumference of your waist, plus 1 foot.

12. Thread the ends of your yarn through some heavy beads (small enough to fit through your ring) and knot off.

13. Wrap the belt around your waist.

14. Pull the beaded end through the ring, and let it hang. The result is a snappy macramé belt.

ANCHOR THE YARN

1.

2.

3.

4.

BASIC SQUARE KNOT

1.

1 2 3 4

2.

4 2 3 1

3.

1 2 3 4

HOW TO
Care for
A FERN

No hippie pad is complete without at least one fern, preferably a Boston fern (popular with hippies because of the Boston's general hardiness).

WHAT YOU NEED

* A basket
* Moss
* Potting soil
* A fern
* A hook screw
* A macramé plant hanger

(continued)

1. Line the basket with moss.

2. Remove the fern from the pot it came in, gently shaking off any loose soil.

3. Place the fern in the basket and fill in the space around the edges with a generous amount of fresh potting soil. Pack the soil lightly with your hands.

4. Water the fern so soil is moist to the touch and leave it to drain in a sink or outdoors for 1 hour before hanging.

5. Screw a hook into the ceiling about 1 foot in from a sunny window. (Be sure you screw into a beam—to find one use your fist to knock on the ceiling until you don't hear a hollow sound.)

6. Place the basket in the plant hanger.

7. Hang the hanger from the hook.

8. Water every 3 to 5 days, when the soil feels dry to the touch or the leaves are beginning to droop.

HINT: TAKE THE FERN DOWN AND WATER IT OVER THE SINK TO AVOID A MESS.

RAPPING WITH YOUR FERN

**Some hippies think that plants grow better if you talk to them.
What do you say to a plant? Here are some conversation starters.**

* **"Your leaves look great today!"**

* **"You look pale. Are you getting enough sun?"**

* **"It's funny, you don't look like a fern."**

* **"I love you!"**

----

*All plants enjoy listening to music. But what sort of music is right for your
plant? Test a few tunes out to see how your plant responds. Does it droop at the
sound of Beethoven and perk up to the growl of Tom Waits? It's possible that
you and your plant won't be able to agree on what music to play. Don't let this
interfere with your relationship. It's OK to play your loud hip-hop, as long as
you rub your plant's leaves and coo at it soothingly.*

(NOTE: IT IS A KNOWN FACT THAT ALMOST ALL SPIDER PLANTS LOVE JONI MITCHELL.)

HOW TO
Tie-Dye
A T-SHIRT

* A 100 percent cotton T-shirt
* Sodium carbonate
* Rubber bands
* Rubber or latex gloves

* Clothing dyes in colors of your choosing
* Plastic squeeze bottles (squeezable ketchup bottles work great)
* Plastic bags or plastic wrap

1. If your T-shirt is new, wash and dry it before starting.

2. Pre-soak your T-shirt for 1 hour in a solution of diluted sodium carbonate (1 cup per gallon of water).

3. Tie your T-shirt using one of the classic tie-dye ties (see facing page) or one of your own design, securing it with rubber bands.

4. Put on the gloves.

5. Mix the dyes. (Follow the directions that come with whatever dyes you choose—remember that adding water to the dye will dilute the color.)

6. Put the dye solutions into the squirt bottles.

7. Apply the dye to your tied T-shirt. One approach is to dye the area between rubber bands one color, then the next area between rubber bands another color. When you are done, no white should be visible. (The dye will not completely penetrate the folds, which will remain white when you unwrap the shirt.)

(continued)

knotting

swirl/spiral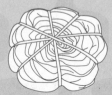

pleats

sunburst

stripes

8. Wrap the T-shirt in plastic wrap or put it in a plastic bag to keep it moist. The fabric must remain wet for the dye to set, at least 2 hours, but preferably 8 to 24 hours. The colors will be richer the longer you leave it.

9. Hand wash your T-shirt, first in cold water, then in warm, then in hot, until no dye runs off in the water. Don't toss it in the washing machine with your blue Moroccan caftan until you're sure it's colorfast.

OTHER THINGS YOU CAN TIE-DYE

* **Tube socks**
* **Flags**
* **Bedspreads**
* **Curtains**
* **Underwear**

CLASSIC TIE-DYE TIES

* **Spiral or starburst:** Determine where you want the center of your spiral to be (say, the chest), and hold the T-shirt in that spot. Twist the fabric around that point, securing it at several points (perhaps six) with rubber bands. Continue twisting and securing until the entire shirt is rolled up.

* **Concentric circles:** Follow the instructions for the spiral, but don't twist the fabric when applying the rubber bands.

* **V pattern:** Fold the T-shirt in half lengthwise. Starting at the bottom corner of the sleeve, fold the fabric in even segments back and forth accordion style. Fasten rubber bands around the fabric as you go to hold it in place.

* **Stripes:** Roll the fabric into a tube, and fasten rubber bands along the length.

HOW TO MAKE PINTO PANTS

My father loved to wear pinto pants. This style, thankfully, did not survive the 1970s. Here's how you do it.

1. Fill a bathtub with warm water.

2. Add 1 cup of bleach to the water.

3. Knot the legs of a pair of dark blue jeans several times.

4. Place the knotted jeans in the water.

5. Let them soak for 2 hours.

6. Remove the jeans, untie the knots, and place the pants in the sun.

7. Let dry.

When the jeans are dry, you will notice that they now have large, unpredictably shaped pale patches where the bleach settled, giving your jeans the appearance of a pinto pony. Why would you want your jeans to look like a pinto pony? I don't know.

PINTO PONY　　　　　　　　**PINTO PANTS**

HOW TO
Make a Skirt
OUT OF A PAIR OF OLD JEANS

Sometimes a pair of cutoffs just won't cut it. For those dressier occasions, try a cut-off skirt. Cutoff skirts are ideal for attending outdoor concerts, graduations, and most summer crafts festivals.

1. Using the scissors, cut the jeans horizontally about 4 inches above the knee. Discard the leg fabric. (When you have fifty of them, you can make a cape!)

2. Cut along the entire inseam. You will now have a denim skirt with a triangular piece missing in the front and back. It will look very immodest.

3. Lay 1 square of fabric facedown inside the skirt so that the fabric fills in the front triangle.

4. Use your pen to trace the two diagonal sides of the triangle on the back side of the square of fabric.

(continued)

1.

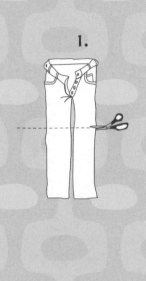

2.

3.

FRONT

BACK

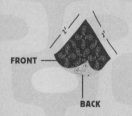

BACK

4.

5.

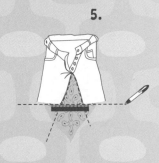

6.

7.

8.

9.

HEM ———

——— "NATURAL LOOK"

5. Use a ruler to draw the bottom of the triangle so that the line is flush with the bottom of the skirt.

6. Remove the fabric. Use your scissors to cut out the shape you have drawn, adding an inch all the way around the outside of the line.

7. Using your sewing machine, sew the fabric in place.

8. Repeat steps 4 through 8 for the back triangle.

9. Hem the entire skirt. Or, if you want a more "natural" look, cut the fabric flush with the bottom edge of the skirt and call it good.

HOW TO GROW AN
Avocado Sprout
FROM A SEED IN A JAR

Why do hippies do this? No one knows. For a while there in 1972, it was difficult to find a hippie windowsill that did not have an avocado seed sprouting in a jar. (Some hippies credit this phenomenon with ending the war in Vietnam.)

WHAT YOU NEED

* **An avocado** * **3 toothpicks** * **A jar**

----

1. Peel and eat the avocado. Save the pit.

2. Let the seed dry for 48 hours.

3. Peel off the papery brown skin.

4. Insert 3 toothpicks equidistant from each other around the middle of the seed, pushing them in far enough to feel securely lodged.

5. Place the seed, pointed end up, in the jar so that the toothpicks rest on the edge of the jar's mouth, suspending the seed.

6. Add warm water to the jar so that the bottom third of the seed is submerged.

7. Put the jar in a warm spot, away from direct sunlight.

8. Check the seed daily, adding warm water to the jar so that the bottom third of the seed is always in water.

9. When the seed begins to sprout roots, move the jar to a windowsill.

10. Soon you will see a stem push up through the pit. When the stem is 3 to 4 inches high, you can plant the seed in soil.

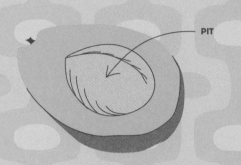

PIT

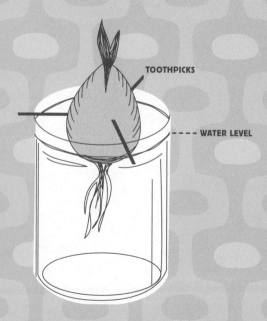

TOOTHPICKS

- - - - WATER LEVEL

HOW TO MAKE AN
Origami Crane

WHAT YOU NEED

* **A square piece of paper (a different color on each side)**

* **Approximately 20 hours**

It pains me to even see the word origami. *As a child I spent days on end holed up in my room trying to fold tiny pieces of colored paper into so-called peace cranes. Rumor had it that if you made one thousand of these things, whatever you wished for would come true. I folded and folded until my fingers cramped and the paper was moist from my sweaty little hands. My complete failure at origami did not prevent origami sets from raining down on me on every possible occasion— I received at least four origami sets a year from ages six to ten. Today, origami remains a popular hippie pastime.*

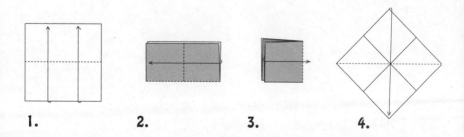

1.　　　　**2.**　　　　**3.**　　　　**4.**

(continued)

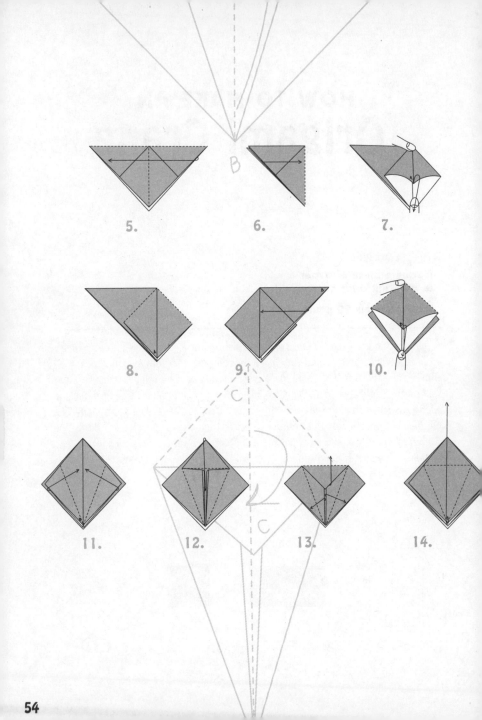

5.

6.

7.

8.

9.

10.

11.

12.

13.

14.

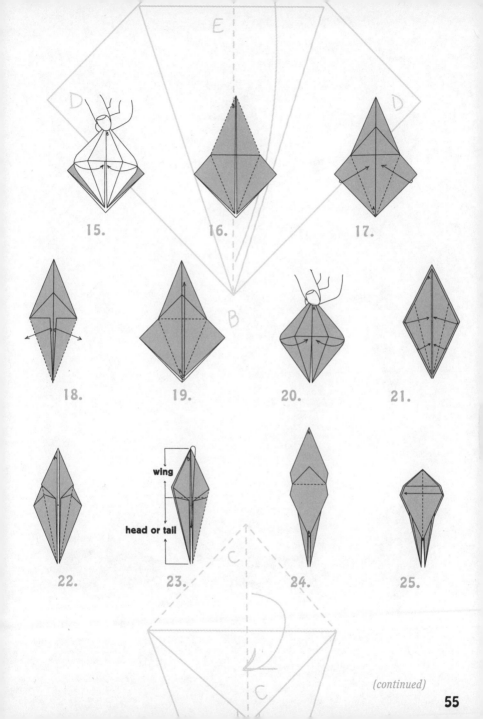

15.

16.

17.

18.

19.

20.

21.

22.

wing

head or tail

23.

24.

25.

(continued)

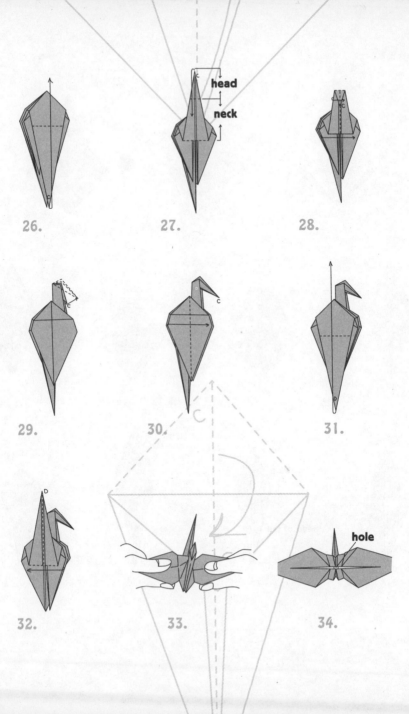

26.

27.

head

neck

28.

29.

30.

31.

32.

33.

34.

hole

HOW TO
Amble

Hippies do not drive if they can possibly walk, or if not walk, bike, or if not bike, unicycle. So how do you know which mode of transportation is appropriate? As a general rule, if your destination is less than three miles away, walk there. If it is less than seven miles away, bike there. If your destination is farther than seven miles away, hitchhike or drive.

Hippies do not walk anywhere fast, and they generally prefer to take a "scenic route," walk on the sunny side of the street, stop and smell the roses, and return stray dogs to their owners. All this can end up adding quite a bit of time to one's journey. This is one of the reasons hippies find it problematic to hold down jobs.

AMBLING TIPS

* Walk barefoot.

* Stay on grass as much as possible.

* Invite a canine companion to accompany you, off leash.

* Notice snails, slugs, blossoms, spider webs, colors, clouds, nests, rocks, nuts, and berries.

* Jaywalk (crosswalks are oppressive).

* Beware hallucinations that might be SUVs, and SUVs that might be hallucinations.

* Play a pennywhistle.

SUPPLIES

Carry a backpack full of essentials: A canteen of tap water, trail mix, the
I Ching, your journal, colored pencils, a Frisbee, patchouli. Remember:
your backpack can be a great place to show off your colorful patches.

OTHER PEOPLE'S YARDS

Some people in Babylon are very uptight about what they perceive as
"trespassing" on their "property." While interesting shortcuts abound,
try to resist traveling through backyards, and if you are going to stop
and rest on a stranger's porch, try to keep it to just a few minutes.

Do not attempt to climb fences. This is how many hippies are hurt.

HOW TO
Hitchhike

1. Move to Northern California.

2. Stand on the side of the street where traffic is headed in the direction you want to go.

3. Make your street-side hand into a fist, and extend your thumb straight up.

4. Extend your arm straight out, perpendicular to the road.

5. Smile.

- -

HITCHHIKING HINTS

* **Try to look more like a college kid and less like Charles Manson.**

* **Wear shoes.**

* **If you are male, find a female to hitchhike with you.**

* **If you are female, find a dog to hitchhike with you.**

* **Do not carry an axe, rifle, or any other kind of large weapon.***

* THIS MAY SEEM PRETTY OBVIOUS, BUT
I ONCE PASSED A HITCHHIKER WHO WAS
CARRYING AN AXE. I'M PRETTY SURE NO
ONE STOPPED FOR HIM.

Hippies used to hitchhike with signs that vaguely indicated where they wanted to be delivered. My parents, for instance, hitchhiked across the country with a sign that read, simply, "East Coast." This doesn't work so well anymore, since most drivers will think to themselves, "But I am not going to the East Coast! I am only going as far as Kansas City." You do not want drivers to think this. You want drivers to think, "What a nice young person. I will take him as close to his destination as I can." So if you are traveling a good distance, figure out the likely destination of most drivers on the road you've chosen, preferably about half a day's drive from where you are right now, and write that location on your sign.

HOW TO
Drive like a Hippie

Some people think that hippie vehicles are a hazard and should not be allowed on the road. In fact, hippie rides are safer than most cars, as they rarely reach speeds over 15 miles per hour.

- Always travel at least five miles under the posted speed limit.

- Tailgate.

- Flash peace signs at other drivers after you cut them off.

- Two words: rolling stop.

- Forget what your destination is.

- Never carry your driver's license.

- Always listen to music either full blast or so low that it can barely be detected. (Don't settle for any song less than eleven minutes long.)

Most people spend a lot of time in their cars. So why do they drive bland sedans or SUV drone-mobiles without any sort of personal expression whatsoever? Two words: resale value. But this is just another way that The Man keeps us slaves to the capitalist machine. And, ha! Hippies do not resell cars. They personalize them and then drive them until they are rusted shells, leaving them along the highway outside Albuquerque. With this radical act, hippies are free to express themselves without being financially punished by Babylon.

NOTE: ANY VEHICLE SHOULD BE OBTAINED BY BARTERING. IF CASH IS NECESSARY, NEVER PAY MORE THAN $750.

SWEET HIPPIE RIDES

* **Volkswagen Microbus** (1942–1971)
* **Volkswagen Beetle** (1950–1965)
* **Volkswagen Squareback** (1962–1973)
* **Volkswagen Fastback** (1962–1973)
* **Volvo sedan** (1950–1965)
* **Saab** (1950–1965)
* **GMC/Chevy or Ford pickup** (1951–1956)
* **Retired mail truck, school bus, hearse, ice cream truck, or repair van**

INTERIOR DECORATIONS

* **Beads**
* **Peace symbol pendants**
* **Sage (to cover odor)**
* **Crystal teardrops, strung on leather straps**
* **Stained-glass pendants, strung on ribbons**
* **Dreamcatchers**
* **A lock of your old lady's hair**

PAINT YOUR VEHICLE! CONSIDER . . .

* **Breaching whales (not "beaching" whales. That would be a bummer.)**
* **Grateful Dead skeletons and/or bears**
* **Flowers**
* **Psychedelic swirls**
* **Airbrushed likeness of Jimi Hendrix, or yourself, or your old lady**

IF YOUR "CAR" IS A BICYCLE

* Spray it with paint (pink, green, or zebra stripes).

* Add streamers to the handle-bars.

* Thread wildflowers between the spokes.

* Find a small child to ride on your handlebars.

* Attach a basket to the front (for carrying produce) and a milk crate to the back (for carrying litters of kittens).

* Add a cheerful-sounding horn.

* Glue tiny plastic farm animals all over the bumpers.

TYPICAL HIPPIE BUMPER STICKERS

* Peace slogans*

* Music slogans

* Marijuana slogans*

* Tolkien quotations

*THESE MAY INCREASE CHANCES OF GETTING PULLED OVER.

NAMING YOUR VEHICLE

All hippie vehicles have a name. (SEE "HOW TO NAME YOUR HIPPIE BABY," P. 30.)

HOW TO
Change the Oil
IN YOUR VW BUS

These directions should work for all pre-1973 Volkswagen buses. Change the oil every three months or three thousand miles, whichever comes first.

WHAT YOU NEED

* **19-mm wrench**
* **A flat pan to collect the drained oil (big enough for 3 quarts)**
* **10-mm wrench**
* **Solvent to wash the oil strainer screen and plate**
* **Oil change gasket kit**
* **2.5 L oil (30W should be fine)**

2.5 liters of oil

flat pan

10-mm wrench

19-mm wrench

oil change gasket kit

1. Take your bus for a drive the length of at least three Grateful Dead songs. This will allow the oil to warm up so you'll be sure to get out all the sludge when you drain it.

2. Park and turn off the bus, and look under it. The oil drain plate is the round plate in the middle underside of the engine or, depending on your model, the middle underside left. There is a large bolt (the drain plug) in the center and 6 nuts spaced around the perimeter.

3. Use the 19-mm wrench and loosen the drain plug until you can turn it by hand. Do not loosen all the way.

4. Place the pan beneath this bolt and continue to loosen until the bolt comes out and the oil starts flowing. **Remember, the oil is hot, so be careful.**

5. Let the oil drain into your pan for 15 minutes.

6. When the oil has drained out, use the 10-mm wrench to undo the 6 nuts holding the oil drain plate in place (keep the nuts and washers in a safe place so you don't lose them). Remove the plate, keeping the pan in place to catch any remaining oil.

7. Remove the screen from the bottom of the engine and wash it in solvent.

8. Wash the plate in solvent, too.

9. Now remove the gaskets from the oil drain plate and from the bottom of the engine where you removed the plate. Dispose of the old gaskets.

10. Put new gaskets on each side of the screen and work it up on the studs. Follow quickly with the clean plate.

11. Replace and tighten the washers and nuts with the 10-mm wrench.

12. Put the drain plug in and tighten it with the 19-mm wrench.

13. Fill the engine with oil. Check under the bus for leaks and tighten drain plug and nuts if necessary.

HOW TO TAKE CARE OF
Birkenstocks

For a group of folks who eschew material goods, a pair of Birkenstocks is a significant investment. Many hippies who do not wash their hair will go to great lengths to extend the life of their footwear.

AVOID INTENSE HEAT

The cork and soles can be damaged by exposure to concentrated heat. Do not leave your Birks in the minibus at Burning Man, and keep them away from the communal bonfire at night. If your shoes become wet while you are cavorting in a stream, allow them to dry slowly, away from sources of heat.

REPAIR WORN SOLES

Don't wait for your soles to wear down to the cork. Have the soles repaired when they have been worn down to about $^{1}/_{8}$ inch, before the cork is damaged.

RINSE OFF SALT

If you walk on the beach in your Birks, be sure to immediately wash off the salt-water residue with fresh water to avoid corrosion.

KEEP TRACK OF YOUR SHOES

Many a hippie has left his Birkenstocks on a porch, beach, or youth hostel stoop, only to have them pinched in short order. If you leave your shoes behind, at least hide them under a towel, bury them in sand (but mark the spot so that you can find them later), or cover them with branches.

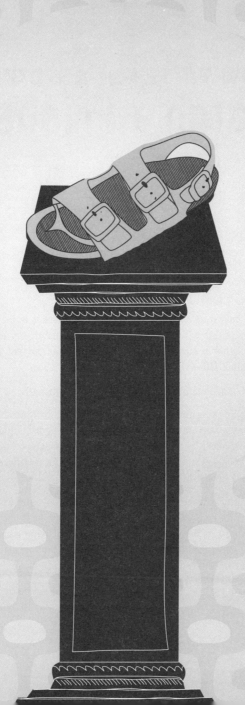

HOW TO TEACH A DOG TO
Catch a Frisbee

* **2 Frisbees** * **A bandanna** * **A dog**

----

1. Buy your dog a Frisbee to have around the house. Let him carry it around, chew on it, wear it as a hat, whatever. The idea here is to let your dog become comfortable with the notion of a Frisbee existing in the world, so that later, when it comes careening toward his head, he will not panic quite so much. This Frisbee will become your "nasty Frisbee."

2. Tie a sporty bandanna around your dog's neck (optional).

3. Find a park (or backyard) with enough open space for your dog to frolic without running into traffic. The park should be dog friendly so that your dog can be off leash, but not so dog friendly that when you throw the Frisbee for *your* dog, seventeen other dogs lunge for it. If you have a fenced-in backyard, all the better.

4. Throw the other Frisbee, the "nice" one, for your dog. You will use the nice Frisbee for training because you will notice that the nasty Frisbee is so chewed up that it defies the laws of physics. Also, using a nice Frisbee will let your dog know that this is a special and important occasion. (Most dogs will chase a Frisbee, especially a nice one. Some will bring it back, but most will simply pick it up and taunt you with it.)

5. Once your dog gets the idea that a thrown Frisbee is something to be caught, start taunting *him* with it. Play tug-of-war. Hold the Frisbee up above your head and encourage your dog to jump for it. Once your dog has mastered jumping for the Frisbee, try dropping it as your dog jumps. Do this until your dog gets used to catching a moving Frisbee.

6. Throw the Frisbee, starting with short tosses, and move on to longer throws as your dog progresses. Praise each catch effusively.

NOTE: YOU CAN ALSO TEACH A SMALL CHILD TO CATCH A FRISBEE USING THIS METHOD.

HOW TO
Make Sand Candles
AS HOLIDAY GIFTS

One of the great joys of being a hippie is its attendant opportunity to thwart the capitalist economic machine. Hippies, as a rule, never, ever give store-bought presents.

WHAT YOU NEED

* **Sand**

* **Broom handle, drinking glass, spoon, or other object for shaping candle mold**

* **Wicks**

* **Skewer**

* **Candle wax, or paraffin**

* **Crayons for color (optional)**

* **Batik cloth**

1. Go to Laguna Beach, California. If you cannot get to Laguna Beach, fill a tall container with sand from a nearby beach or local schoolyard sandbox. Some "sand candle geeks" insist on using store-bought sand, but of course hippies do not buy store-bought sand when there is perfectly good sand to be gotten without supporting the war machine. (Just be sure to sift the cat poop out of any sandbox sand.)

2. Add enough water to the sand so that it holds its shape when you press it together with your hands.

(continued)

3. Dig a hole in the sand in the shape you want your candle to be. You can use a broom handle to make the shape of a tall, thin pillar candle or a small glass to make the shape of a votive candle. Or you can get fancy and use a spoon to try to create a likeness of Janis Joplin.

4. When your sand mold is finished, hold a piece of wick over the approximate center and secure it to a skewer positioned horizontally over the hole. The part tied to the skewer will be the top of the wick; be sure that the other end reaches the bottom center of your sand mold and does not drift to the side of your candle.

5. Melt the wax in a double boiler (or in an old coffee can over a campfire if you're on the beach). Add unwrapped crayons to the wax for color, if you like, continuing to heat the wax until the crayons melt. Carefully pour the wax into the hole.

6. Let the wax cool and harden overnight.

7. Snip the wick about an inch above the top of the wax. Slip your hands under the candle and gently lift it out. Brush off any excess sand.

8. Wrap in batik cloth.

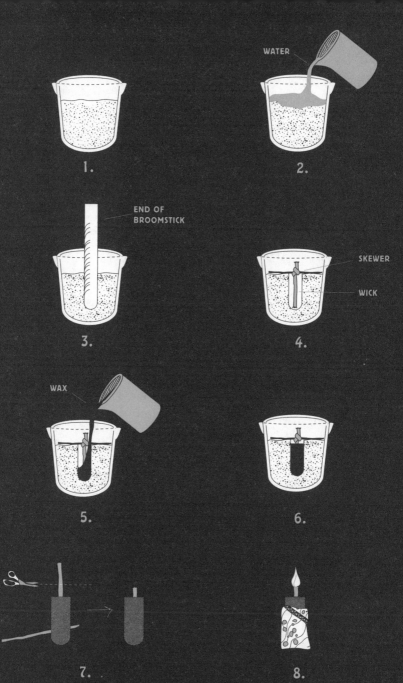

WATER

1.

2.

END OF
BROOMSTICK

SKEWER

WICK

3.

4.

WAX

5.

6.

7.

8.

HOW TO
Draw Psychedelic Letters

Hippies have the grooviest lettering style of all the counterculture movements. The psychedelic free-form bubble lettering popularized by the Haight-Ashbury concert posters of the mid to late 1960s is an art that takes much practice to replicate. Each artist brings his or her own interpretation, and no hippie lettering is the same. But there are some tricks.

- -

THE TRICKS

* **Imagine that the letters are expanding outward into the universe.**

* **Don't use right angles, ever.**

* **Connect each letter to the one next to it.**

* **Vary letter sizes.**

* **Do not use punctuation.**

HOW AND WHEN TO
Flash a Peace Sign

HOW TO FLASH A PEACE SIGN

1. With palm facing out, fold your pinky finger and ring finger toward your palm, holding them in place with your thumb.

2. Extend your index finger and middle finger in a V shape.

WHEN TO FLASH A PEACE SIGN

* In greeting

* In all photographs

* To another driver, after committing a traffic violation

* When faced with members of the U.S. armed forces

* When passing other hippies

* After giving a speech

* In farewell

WHEN NOT TO FLASH A PEACE SIGN

* When being questioned by the police

* When encountering a deaf person (in American Sign Language this is the sign for the letter V, and will cause confusion)

peace sign   Mercedes-Benz logo

THE PEACE SYMBOL (YOUNGER READERS MIGHT MISTAKE IT FOR A MERCEDES LOGO) WAS DESIGNED BY GERALD HOLTOM TO SERVE AS THE SYMBOL FOR THE CAMPAIGN FOR NUCLEAR DISARMAMENT IN 1958.

"N"   "D"

THE SYMBOL IS BASED ON THE SEMAPHORE SIGNALS FOR THE LETTERS *N* (NUCLEAR) AND *D* (DISARMAMENT). HOLTOM ALSO LATER DESCRIBED THE SYMBOL AS AN IMAGE OF "AN INDIVIDUAL IN DESPAIR, WITH PALMS STRETCHED OUTWARDS AND DOWNWARDS IN THE MANNER OF GOYA'S PEASANT BEFORE THE FIRING SQUAD."

HOW TO SIT IN THE LOTUS POSITION

1. Sit on the floor in a cross-legged position.

2. Slowly pull your left foot onto your right thigh, sole up.

3. Slowly pull your right foot onto your left thigh, sole up.

4. Sit up straight.

5. Remember that pain is a transcendent pleasure on the road to enlightenment.

HOW TO
Meditate

1. Find a quiet place.

2. Sit up straight in a comfortable position, either in a chair or on the floor in the lotus position.

3. Close your eyes. (You may meditate with your eyes open or closed, but people who meditate with their eyes open tend to be scary.)

4. Focus on your breathing. Breathe in through your nose, and out through your mouth. Imagine your breath fanning out of your mouth, ridding your body of heat and toxins.

5. You may notice that your mind is full of clutter. You may start to think of things you didn't know you cared about, like the name of your fourth-grade teacher, your favorite Peter Fonda film, or the lyrics to "Yellow Submarine." Let these thoughts pass through your mind. Don't judge them. Stay focused on your breath. Visualize your forehead as a piece of smooth silk. Continue sitting and focusing for 10 or 15 minutes.

6. Bliss out.

7. Repeat daily.

IF YOU MEDITATE REGULARLY, YOU WILL NOTICE
THAT YOUR MIND WILL BECOME MORE QUIET.
AND YOUR NOSE WON'T ITCH AS MUCH.

HOW TO
Howl at the Moon

Don't wait for a full moon! Moon howling can occur at any time of the month, as long as the moon is visible in the sky.

----

1. Surrender your self-consciousness.

2. Lean your head back.

3. Look at the moon.

4. Howl in a lupine manner.

I did not howl at the moon until I was in college, when I went to an Earth First rally. The speaker was Dave Foreman, an environmentalist warrior known for, among other things, his howling. We were all crammed in a university lecture hall in Orange County, California. We did not feel one with the woods. Foreman howled. We all looked at him. Foreman howled again. We all looked at each other. A few people headed for the door. Foreman kept howling. Within moments we were all howling like madcap werewolves.

HOW TO
Choose a Mantra

Some people employ mantras while meditating. A mantra is a word that you say over and over in your mind, until the word becomes meaningless and your mind empties of distracting thoughts. You'll want to choose a word that rolls off the tongue. For instance, say "puddle" rather than "Schenectady." Many meditating hippies choose mantras such as "Om shanti," drawn from languages that they do not speak, since these don't carry as much semantic baggage. Once you pick a mantra, keep it to yourself. People say that it loses power if you spread it around. Also, other people don't care.

SHOULD I SAY MY MANTRA OUT LOUD?

Everyone who meditates using a mantra is soon faced with a dilemma: chant the mantra out loud, or chant the mantra in your head? Of course you should do what's comfortable, taking into account that you have neighbors.

SOME POPULAR MANTRAS

* **Om**
* **Om Shanti Shanti Shanti**
* **Hare Krishna**
* **Om Namah Shivaya**
* **Your girlfriend's or boyfriend's first name**
* **Shazam**
* **D-u-u-u-u-de**

mountain pose

arm stretch

fold forward

downward-facing dog

plank

transition

upward-facing dog

downward-facing dog

fold forward

arm stretch

mountain pose

HOW TO DO A
Sun Salutation

The salutation is a series of yoga poses done in a fluid manner, with special attention paid to breathing. Sun salutations vary depending on the instructor and type of yoga. Many instructors believe that the sun salutation is the most important series of poses a student can do. To complete the sun salutation, move through the following series of poses in the order they are shown. Then repeat several times. Remember, yoga is not a contest—just complete the pose to the best of your ability.

I went to a clothing-optional daycare where we did yoga at recess every day. If you choose to do this outdoors, remember: do not look directly into the sun unless you are wearing eye protection.

HOW TO FIND
Spiritual
Enlightenment

Most hippies' belief systems fall somewhere between atheism and paganism, which leaves a lot of ground for exploration, and many hippies choose to mix and match their favorite parts of different faiths. My mother, who was raised Catholic, experimented with several spiritual leanings before settling on Buddhism. We once had a séance at our house attended by the Archangel Michael (he was nice). Mom also had flings with Transcendental Meditation, astrology, and reincarnation.

WHAT MY MOTHER LOOKED FOR ON THE ROAD TO ENLIGHTENMENT

* **Something that would not require gathering with others at a specific location at regular intervals**

* **Something that would not be a "buzz kill"**

* **Guidance, rather than dogma**

* **Something that Mia Farrow had dabbled in**

* **Something that would not require giving money to a bearded man**

* **Cherry incense**

* **Chanting**

* **No (or very little) dancing**

* **Buddhism**
* **Taoism**
* **Hinduism**
* **Astrology**
* **Animism**
* **Transcendentalism**
* **I Ching**
* **New Ageism**
* **Ancient Judaism**
* **The Church of the Sub-Genius**
* **Native American spiritualism**
* **Cults**
* **Tarot**

* **India**
* **Marin County, California**
* **The woods**
* **On-line**
* **Rock concerts**

HOW TO
Start a Commune

* A house, preferably with several outbuildings
* A group of open-minded, perfectly matched people with complementary skills, goals, and life philosophies
* A goat
* A chore sign-up sheet
* A casual relationship with the notion of privacy
* "On Liberty" by John Stuart Mill
* The collected works of Karl Marx and Friedrich Engels
* A natural inclination toward egalitarianism
* A belief in the inherent benefits of "intentional communities"

----

1. Move into house.

2. Get along.

3. Garden.

THE RULE PARADOX

Rules are naturally a touchy subject among hippies. If you are starting a commune, you'll need some guidelines in order to prevent complete chaos, but it is best to keep them to a few, if only to avoid the several day-long house meetings required to decide which rules to make and how to follow them. There were two rules on the farm we lived on when I was a kid. The first was "Everyone gives something, and everyone gets something back." If you didn't do your part (e.g., you refused to help paint the porch, or you kicked the puppies out of the shed so you could park your motorcycle), you were asked to leave. The second rule was "Don't let the dogs into the sheep pen." This was the one I had trouble remembering.

Once you accept that everyone has an equal responsibility to share in the commune chores, you can immediately begin trying to get out of them. The best way? Have a baby! My mother was accused of having me so she could get out of doing the dishes.

GARDENING—GOLF FOR HIPPIES

Hippies love to garden, and there is nothing better for a commune than a good-sized vegetable patch. A few tomato plants, some basil, and some rhubarb will keep hippies busy for the better part of a summer. Everyone can participate in the garden's care and harvest. Because all residents are participating, the garden is truly a product of the community and a central element of commune life. Also, a bountiful garden can feed a bevy of hungry hippies for several months—longer if produce is jarred or frozen.

Television is generally discouraged in communes, mostly because the number of people makes it hard to decide what to watch. We did not have a television at the farm until 1973, when the group decided that they wanted to watch the Watergate hearings. A small black-and-white television was purchased, but my mother decreed that it was not to be allowed inside the house, "on principle." An extension cord was strung out the kitchen window and the TV was set up on the porch, where my parents and their friends watched it that summer as they worked in the garden. Until I was nine, my mother refused to buy me anything that was advertised on TV. I had a hell of a time convincing her that the Barbie doll phenomenon was all the result of word of mouth.

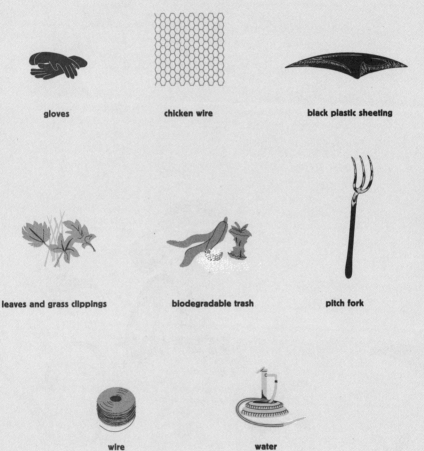

gloves

chicken wire

black plastic sheeting

leaves and grass clippings

biodegradable trash

pitch fork

wire

water

HOW TO BUILD A
Compost Pile

* **Materials for making a compost bin (wire, chicken wire, black plastic sheeting)**

* **Lots of leaves**

* **A garden hose**

* **Biodegradable trash**

* **A hoe or pitchfork**

----

1. Select a shady spot outdoors where water does not collect when it rains, far enough away from your house (and your punk rock neighbors') so that the smell won't keep anyone up at night.

2. Build your compost bin (see illustration, page 99). A good size is 4 feet wide by 4 feet tall, big enough to contain an average household's biodegradables and allow the pile to "cook," but not so big that you lose your backyard.

3. Cover the bottom of the bin with a 6-inch layer of leaves. It does not matter what kind. Water enthusiastically.

4. Add a 2-inch layer of grass clippings and/or kitchen scraps mixed with soil.

5. Using a hoe, mix this layer into the layer of wet leaves below it. Water enthusiastically.

6. Top with a 2-inch layer of leaves.

7. Add layers if ingredients are available. The topmost layer should consist of at least 4 inches of leaves to cover all food materials.

(continued)

8. Check the pile every week and use a garden hose to keep it sponge damp. Cover it with a tarp if you live in a rainy climate; if the pile gets too wet (or too dry), this will slow the decay process.

9. Turn the pile twice a month using a garden hoe or pitchfork. The center of the pile will "cook," reaching temperatures of up to 160°F. It will smell ripe, it will often emit steam when you turn it, and it will be warm to the touch, even through gloves. If the pile is not heating up, add a 2-inch layer of nitrogen (commonly known as cow manure) and stir it into the pile with your hoe.

10. Add more to the pile as you want or need to, but always be sure to turn the pile when you do, so that the new stuff is underneath. As composters say, brown always goes on top of green.

11. Finished compost is dark and crumbly, looking and smelling like rich soil. It can take as little as 2 weeks or as long as 3 months for the compost to reach this stage. A wheelbarrow and pitchfork work well for extracting.

ITEMS TO INCLUDE IN YOUR PILE

* What can you compost? Basically anything organic in its natural form that hasn't been chemically treated...

* Yard waste (grass clippings, leaves, etc.)

* Wood ashes

* Kitchen waste (coffee grounds, eggshells, leftover millet casserole, etc.)

ITEMS TO AVOID

* Meat and bones (they are hard to break down both in your colon and in your compost pile)

* Cat or dog feces (too rich in nitrogen)

* Ashes from charcoal (these introduce petroleum by-product derivatives into the soil)

* Paint

* Diapers

* Beer cans

* You get the idea

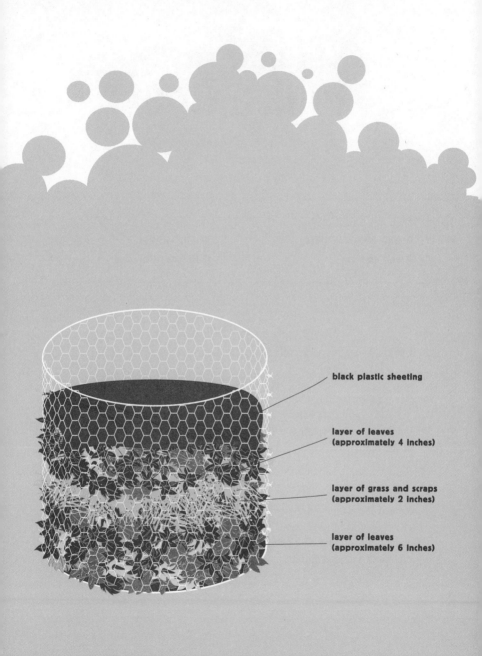

black plastic sheeting

layer of leaves
(approximately 4 inches)

layer of grass and scraps
(approximately 2 inches)

layer of leaves
(approximately 6 inches)

HOW TO
Milk a Goat

WHAT YOU NEED

* **A pail of warm water**
* **A sea sponge**

* **A milk bucket**
* **One goat (female)**

HOW TO MILK

1. Place the pail of warm water under the goat's udder.

2. Use the sponge to clean off the goat's teats.

3. Clasp your thumb and index finger around one of the goat's teats.

4. Squeeze the teat shut with your thumb and index finger at a point close to the udder, and then open your grip slightly. By clamping your thumb and index finger, you create a valve that allows milk to be captured at the bottom of the teat.

5. Slide the same hand down the length of the teat to squeeze the milk from the bottom of the teat into the milk bucket.

6. Repeat the clasping and squeezing process until you have the amount of milk you want. Proficient goat milkers will milk two teats at the same time and alternate to other teats when the stream of milk diminishes to intermittent spurts.

7. Filter the milk using cheesecloth or a coffee filter. This will strain out any hair or dirt that may have contaminated the milk. Store the milk in a mason jar with a tight-sealing lid.

8. Refrigerate and drink. Unpasteurized goat milk should keep fresh in the fridge for about one week.

Milking can be a very intimate experience between you and your goat. Make it memorable. Talk to your goat in calming tones. Thank her for her milk, and tell her how much you respect her.

We had two goats when I was a kid: Full Moon and Nelly. I was weaned on Full Moon's milk. To this day I still can't drink cow's milk (it just doesn't have the love in it).

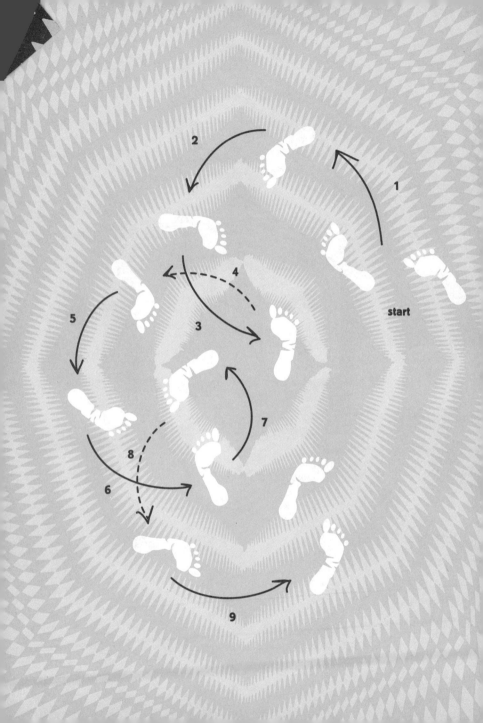

HOW TO
Dance
LIKE A HIPPIE

It is best to dance like a hippie outdoors on soft ground. If you get dizzy and fall, it will hurt less if you do not fall on concrete. This dance is most effective if you are wearing a wide, flowing skirt.

---

1. Take off your shoes.

2. Put your head back.

3. Close your eyes.

4. Extend your arms straight out from your sides.

5. Spin.

6. Repeat as necessary.

HOW TO
Celebrate May Day
LIKE A HIPPIE

May Day has both pagan roots and socialist roots. It also has flowers. It is hard to say which of these attracts hippies most.

1. Prepare your May Pole. Some hippies like to "sacrifice" a living tree for this rite (cutting off low-hanging limbs to make the tree a "pole"), but an old-fashioned, freestanding flagpole will work just as well. If no flagpole or telephone pole is available, any sort of tall, pole-like thing that can be stuck in the ground will work. Fifteen feet is usually tall enough.

2. Tie pretty-colored streamers, one for each guest, to the top of the pole. Each streamer should be one and a half times the height of the pole (e.g., if your pole is 15 feet tall, then each of your streamers should be $22\frac{1}{2}$ feet long).

(continued)

3. Dig a hole in the ground with your posthole digger. It should be a few inches wider than the base of the pole, and deep enough that the pole will not fall and injure innocent hippie children. Make sure there's enough open space all around the pole so that people can walk around it holding the end of the streamers without bumping into rocks, bushes, or other objects.

4. Stick the pole in the ground, and pack dirt tightly around the base. Test to make sure the pole does not wobble perilously.

5. Gather a group of friends and neighbors 'round the May Pole.

6. Ask them to don flower wreathes and crowns (SEE "HOW TO MAKE A DANDELION CROWN," PAGE 110).

7. Give each person one end of a streamer.

8. Instruct them to "dance around the May Pole."

9. The streamers will weave around the pole as your guests frolic and, if you've all been on-task, they will form a decorative braid down the length of the pole when you are done.

10. Now make a bonfire and sing.

.YOU CAN ALSO CELEBRATE MAY DAY WITH A PARADE.
IT IS A LITTLE-KNOWN FACT THAT HIPPIES *LOVE* PARADES.

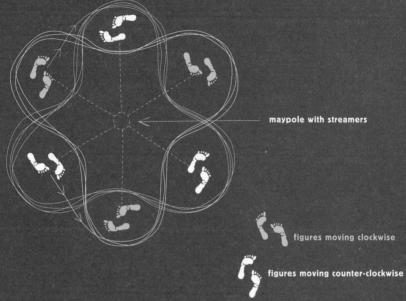

maypole with streamers

figures moving clockwise

figures moving counter-clockwise

THE DANCE

1. Each person holds the end of a streamer and stands in a circle around the May Pole.

2. Everyone faces the May Pole.

3. Every other person turns to their left.

4. The remaining people turn to their right.

5. The left-facing people will dance clockwise around the pole; the right-facing people will dance counterclockwise.

6. The left-facing people will dance to the right around the right-facing people, and to the left around the left-facing people.

7. The right-facing people will dance to the left around the left-facing people and to the right around the right-facing people.

8. This is a lot easier than it sounds.

HOW TO MAKE A
Dandelion Crown

You may know this as a "daisy chain." My mother taught me to do it using dandelions. I think this may have been a yard-maintenance strategy on her part.

WHAT YOU NEED

* **25 to 30 blooming (yellow) dandelions**
* **A fingernail**
* **A rag or washcloth**

---

1. Pick dandelions from your yard or a nearby meadow. Pick the flowers close to the root, so you have a lot of stem to work with.

2. Use your fingernail to make a $1/2$-inch-long slit all the way through each stem. Make the slit close to the head of the dandelion, so your crown will be dense with flowers.

3. Insert the stem of another dandelion into the slit you've created, and pull it through. Now slit the stem of that dandelion and insert the stem of another dandelion.

4. Continue this process until your chain is the length you need.

5. When the chain looks the right crown size for your head, make a slit that is about twice as long as the others on the stem of your last flower and fit the entire head of your first flower through it. Pull gently to tighten.

6. Dandelion goo is sticky and the yellow pollen gets everywhere. Wipe your hands with a rag or washcloth when you're done.

OTHER THINGS YOU CAN MAKE OUT OF DANDELIONS

* **Anklets**
* **Necklaces**
* **Bracelets**
* **Boutonnieres**
* **Bouquets**
* **Wine**

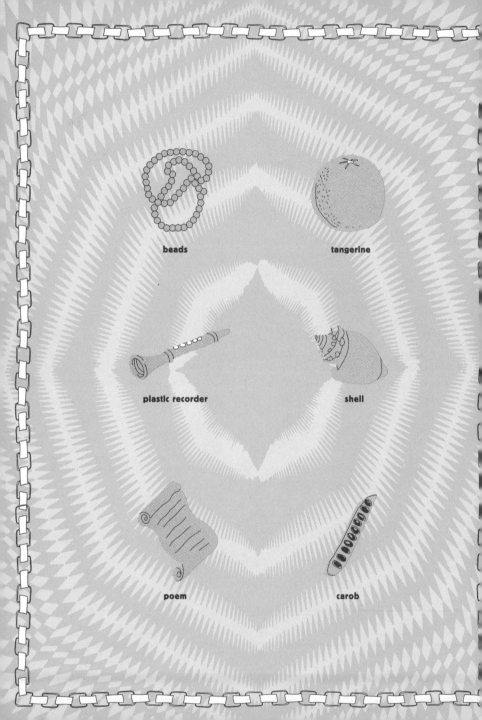

beads

tangerine

plastic recorder

shell

poem

carob

HOW TO CELEBRATE
Your Birthday
LIKE A HIPPIE

THINGS TO DO

* Watch *Free to Be You and Me.*

* Make and hang construction-paper chains.

* Make and wear dandelion crowns (SEE PAGE 110).

* Throw a costume party—perhaps a fantasy theme?

* Make your birthday party a "Save the Seals" benefit.

* Put on a puppet show.

* Do cartwheels.

* Do partner yoga.

* Have guests check their watches and shoes at the door.

PARTY FAVORS

* Beads

* Carob anything

* Tangerines

* Seashells

* Plastic recorders

* Wendell Berry poems written on handmade paper and tied up in small scrolls

HOW TO MAKE A
Vegan Chocolate
BIRTHDAY CAKE
(SERVES 8)

WHAT YOU NEED

- 2 cups brown sugar
- 1 3/4 cups whole-wheat flour
- 3/4 cup unsweetened cocoa powder
- 1 1/2 teaspoons baking soda
- 1 teaspoon salt
- 1 cup soy milk
- 1/2 cup vegetable oil
- 2 teaspoons vanilla extract
- 1 cup boiling water

----

1. Preheat oven to 350°F.

2. Combine the brown sugar, flour, cocoa powder, baking soda, and salt in a bowl.

3. Add the soy milk, oil, and vanilla and beat for 2 minutes.

4. Stir in the boiling water.

5. Pour into an 8-inch square cake pan.

6. Bake 35 to 40 minutes.

7. Allow cake to cool. The cake is done when a toothpick stuck into the center of the cake comes out free of crumbs.

tempeh

STUFF TO DO
Around a Campfire

Every hippie eventually finds him- or herself sitting around a campfire. Hippies are drawn to campfires like moths to a flame. But then what?

---

* Drum.

* Play harmonica.

* Sing "We Shall Overcome" in three-part harmony.

* See if you can name all the bands that played at Woodstock.

* See if you can name all the bands that played at Woodstock in the order they went on.

* Burn incense.

* Plot the revolution.

* Give each other henna tattoos.

* Tell Peace Corps stories.

When I was in the fifth grade my mother decided that we should move to an American Indian reservation "for the experience." We rented a little house on Gooseberry Point in the Lummi reservation near Bellingham, Washington. The "Point" was a small spit of land on the Bay overlooking Lummi Island. We lived across the street from the water, and each night would pack up a bowl of basil pesto pasta, build a fire on the beach, and eat oceanside. We did this every night until the first winter, when the spit flooded and we had to be rescued by a man in a rowboat. As he rowed us to safety, we passed our front porch, which had broken free and was now floating down the street. After we moved back to Bellingham, we still made the half-hour trek back to the beach once a week for several months to eat dinner by campfire.

HOW TO PLAY
"Kumbaya"
ON A GUITAR

SLOW   Key: D

Kum–ba – ya, my Lord,____ Kum–ba – ya. _____ Kum– ba –

ya, my Lord,___ Kum–ba – ya. _____ Kum– ba – ya, my Lord,_

__ Kum–ba – ya. _____ Oh, Lord, Kum–ba – ya. _____

Someone's singing Lord, Kumbaya (3) Oh, Lord, Kumbaya

Kumbaya, my Lord, Kumbaya (3) Oh, Lord, Kumbaya

Someone's praying Lord, Kumbaya (3) Oh, Lord, Kumbaya

Kumbaya, my Lord, Kumbaya (3) Oh, Lord, Kumbaya

Someone's sleeping Lord, Kumbaya (3) Oh, Lord, Kumbaya

Kumbaya, my Lord, Kumbaya (3) Oh, Lord, Kumbaya

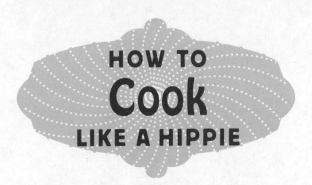

HOW TO
Cook
LIKE A HIPPIE

"OREGANO" BROWNIES
(SERVES 10)

WHAT YOU NEED

* $1/_2$ cup butter
* 2 ounces unsweetened chocolate
* 1 cup sugar
* 2 eggs, well beaten

* $1/_2$ teaspoon vanilla
* $3/_4$ cup flour
* $1/_4$ teaspoon salt
* $1/_8$ ounce "oregano," chopped

1. Preheat oven to 350°F.

2. Melt butter and chocolate together in a large saucepan over low heat.

3. Remove the saucepan from the heat and stir in remaining ingredients.

4. Pour mixture into a greased 8-inch square pan.

5. Bake for 25 to 30 minutes.

6. Let cool.

7. Cut into squares.

8. Serve and enjoy.

FREEZER PESTO
(MAKES 1 CUP)

WHAT YOU NEED

* **3 cups fresh basil leaves, loosely packed**
* **1/3 cup pine nuts**
* **1/2 cup grated Parmesan cheese**

* **3 garlic cloves, chopped**
* **1/2 cup olive oil**
* **Salt and ground black pepper to taste**

---

1. Process all ingredients in a blender or food processor.

2. Freeze the pesto.

NOTE: PESTO, NICELY JARRED, MAKES A LOVELY SOLSTICE OR HOSTESS GIFT.

America has hippies to thank for the popularity of basil pesto. Now firmly under the culinary stewardship of the chardonnay-sipping crowd, pesto was first championed by hippies. It was green, and we liked it. It was always homemade. At the end of the garden season, my mother would make one last vast batch with all the basil that was left and then freeze it to last us through the winter. We ate it on pasta, toast, sandwiches, baked potatoes, pizza, foccacia, and quesadillas, and in vinaigrette on our salads. As far as she was concerned, a meal without pesto was an opportunity wasted.

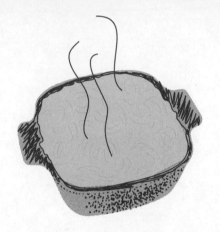

MILLET CASSEROLE
(SERVES 15)

WHAT YOU NEED

- 3 cups uncooked millet
- 1 tablespoon olive oil
- 2 medium onions, diced
- 3 celery stalks, sliced
- 1 cup cooked chickpeas

- 5 cups water
- 1 teaspoon salt
- 2 cups broccoli, chopped
- Grated Parmesan and provolone
- Parsley, minced, for garnish

Millet casserole was a staple at the farm because it was easy to make, and this recipe, when doubled, could feed up to twenty hungry hippies. None of the men liked it because, frankly, millet casserole is not that good. But the women were a little fed up with having to do so much cooking, so they made it a lot. Many of these women went on to join the feminist movement.

A helpful suggestion from my father: If you have to eat millet, eat it with a lot of cheese, and slather it with butter.

1. Rinse and drain millet. (A strainer lined with cheesecloth or a dishtowel works great.)

2. Dry-roast millet in a heavy skillet for 6 minutes over high heat, stirring constantly, until the millet smells nutty and starts to turn a golden brown.

3. Remove skillet from heat.

4. Heat oil in a large saucepan over medium heat and sauté onions for 2 minutes, until they soften.

5. Add celery and sauté for 5 minutes, stirring often.

6. Add chickpeas, water, and salt. Bring to a boil.

7. Stir in millet and return to a boil. Reduce heat, cover, and simmer for 20 minutes.

8. Add broccoli and continue to cook for 5 minutes.

9. Add cheese to taste.

10. While mixture is hot, press firmly into a 9-inch cake pan.

11. Sprinkle with parsley, cut into wedges or squares, and serve.

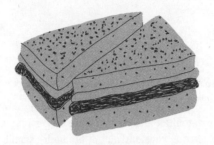

PEANUT BUTTER AND
HONEY SANDWICH
(SERVES 1)

WHAT YOU NEED

* **A butter knife**
* **1 tablespoon all-natural, unsweetened, organic peanut butter**
* **2 slices homemade whole-wheat bread**
* **1 tablespoon honey**

Small children denied white sugar will inevitably go nuts for honey—it's sweet, and, deprived of sugar, the kids don't know any better. Peanut butter and honey sandwiches were always a treat, wrapped in wax paper—this was deemed more environmentally friendly than plastic bags or plastic wrap—and secured with a rubber band. The bread, hand cut from the loaf, was misshapen and full of seeds, raisins, and whatever else was lying around the kitchen. This, combined with the millet, led to extremely healthy and regular bowel movements.

1. Use a butter knife to spread an even coat of peanut butter on one side of a slice of bread.

2. Clean the knife.

3. Spread an even coat of honey on one side of another piece of bread.

4. Place the bread with the peanut butter on it, peanut butter side down, on top of the bread with the honey on it, honey side up, so that the honey and the peanut butter come together.

5. Slice the sandwich from one corner to the opposite corner so that you have two triangular pieces.

6. Eat the sandwich.

tempeh

HOW TO
Grow Tempeh
IN YOUR BATHTUB

Sure, you can buy tasty meatless products at almost all grocery stores, but why would you do that when you can spend hours tediously making your own?

WHAT YOU NEED

* **2 $\frac{1}{2}$ cups whole soybeans**
* **Grain mill or food processor (optional)**
* **2 tablespoons white vinegar**
* **1 teaspoon tempeh starter (a spore mixture that contains the seeds of the fungal culture—it can be ordered over the Internet or purchased at a natural food store)**
* **4 re-sealable plastic bags**
* **Hammer**
* **Small nail**
* **Bathtub**
* **Space heater**
* **Thermometer**

soybeans

1. Split the soybeans. You can do this with a loosely set grain mill or food processor or, if you do not have a grain mill or food processor, by squeezing them using a kneading motion, cracking each bean in half. I heartily recommend using a food processor set on a low speed.

2. In a large pot, soak the soybeans in 8 cups of water for 6 to 18 hours. Stir gently, so the hulls rise to the surface, then pour off the water and hulls. Keep re-adding water and pouring off the hulls until you've drained off as many hulls as seems feasible.

3. Add enough water back into the pot to cover the beans. Add the vinegar and cook for 25 to 30 minutes over medium heat. Drain the water and heat the beans in the pot over medium heat for a few minutes until they are dry, stirring constantly.

4. Allow the beans to cool down to room temperature.

5. Sprinkle the soybeans with 1 teaspoon tempeh starter. Mix with a clean spoon for about 1 minute to distribute the starter evenly.

6. Place the plastic bags in a stack and, using a hammer and clean nail, poke small holes all over the bags about $1/4$ inch apart. A fork will also work.

7. Divide the soybeans among the bags and seal them. Press flat, making sure that the thickness of the beans in each bag is about $1/2$ inch.

8. Spread the packed bags out in your empty bathtub. Using the space heater, heat the room to between 86 and 90°F (this is the optimum spore-producing temperature). If you live in Florida and don't have air conditioning, you can skip the space heater.

9. About 24 to 36 hours later, the bags should be filled completely with white mycelium, and you'll see gray spores poking through the holes in the plastic. The tempeh can be eaten immediately. It will also last in the fridge for about a week.

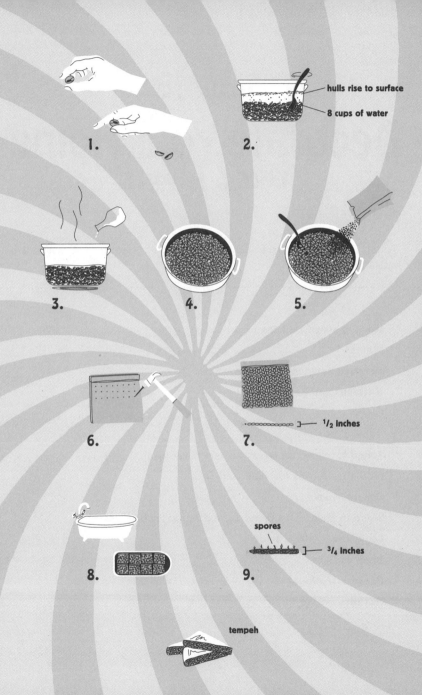

1.

2. hulls rise to surface
8 cups of water

3.

4.

5.

6.

7. ⌐ 1/2 inches

8.

9. spores
⌐ 3/4 inches

tempeh

HOW TO
Decorate Your Home
LIKE A HIPPIE

For a culture that values nonattachment, hippies like to surround themselves with a whole lot of stuff.

NECESSITIES

* **Wood beaded curtains**
* **Plants**
* **Macramé hanging-plant holders**
* **Macramé wall hangings**
* **Loom**
* **Political posters**
* **Found furniture** (SEE HOW TO DUMPSTER DIVE, P. 134)
* **Indian tapestries for walls and sofa**
* **Oriental rugs**
* **Wooden fruit crates** (used as end tables or bookcases)
* **Cable-spool coffee table**
* **Batik curtains**
* **Peacock feathers**
* **Mattress on the floor**

* **Anything wicker**
* **Art you've made, traded for at craft fairs, or purchased at thrift stores**
* **Musical instruments (e.g., banjo, guitar, out-of-tune piano, recorder, harmonica, bongo drums, and sitar)**
* **Quilts (can be hung in doorways in winter for warmth or tucked over torn sofa cushions)**
* **Wine bottles made into candle holders or vases**
* **Pottery wheel**
* **Candles (minimum four per room)**
* **Woodstove or fireplace (does not have to be operational)**
* **Mobiles (the bigger, the better)**
* **Mismatched dishes, silverware, cloth napkins**
* **Jam jars used as drinking glasses**
* **Chopsticks and wooden spoons**
* **Ceramic wind chimes**
* **Bright-colored walls (royal purple, tangerine orange, Chinese red, or electric blue)**
* **Murals**

Why not build an outhouse? The first winter my parents and their friends lived on the farm, all the pipes froze. "Going with the flow," they slapped a strip of duct tape over the toilet, dug a hole for an outhouse, and built an outbuilding over the top. Every summer after that—long after indoor plumbing was functional again— they threw an outhouse party and invited all their friends to come fill in the old hole, dig another, and drag the outbuilding over to cover the new hole.

HOW TO
Dumpster Dive

Dumpster diving has always been one of my favorite hippie pastimes. If you live in Manhattan, where people often leave perfectly good furniture out on the curb and where it is perfectly acceptable for other people to cart it home, you are probably already comfortable with this concept. Others might find it icky. So let's get one thing straight: There is nothing wrong with taking someone else's trash. You'll be amazed at how many treasures are lurking under a layer of takeout Pad Thai and old cottage-cheese containers.

1. Identify your target neighborhood. Concentrate on areas where young people rent. Stay away from wealthy neighborhoods. It is a surprising fact that rich people do not throw good stuff away. They give their trash to charity and deduct it on their tax returns.

2. Determine when trash day is in your target neighborhood (by observation, or by calling the city).

3. The night before trash day ("Trash Eve") drive your VW bus slowly through your target neighborhood.

4. When you spot a dumpster or trash pile that is teeming with bounty, approach it cautiously. (**Do not climb in the dumpster.** Dumpsters can be very dangerous and also dirty.) Bring a footstool so that you can get a good vantage point for sifting. Stay away from clothing, sealed trash bags, and diapers.

5. When you see something you like, carefully free it from the dumpster and load it in the back of your bus.

6. Continue cruising and repeat.

CORRECT

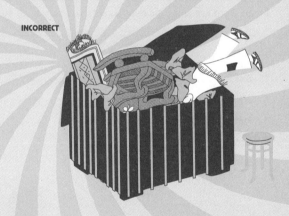

INCORRECT

COLLEGE TOWNS

If you live in a college town, you're in luck! College students are notorious among hippies for their wanton display of "nonattachment" to the material world. Just wait until the week after school gets out for the summer and cruise by dumpsters behind student housing. You will likely find stereo equipment, computers, couches, perfectly good "water pipes," and all manner of stuff that is too big or awkward to haul home to Mom and Dad's in the back of a Civic. If you do not live in a college town, you will have to be a bit more vigilant.

HOW TO
Clean Your House
LIKE A HIPPIE

Hippies are not generally known for their sparkling-clean abodes. This is not due to a lack of effort but instead is due to the hippies' commitment to using nontoxic house-cleaning products. These days, natural cleaning supplies can be purchased at your local health food store, but if you want to save a little bread, here are some cleaning agents you can make yourself.

WHAT YOU NEED

* **Baking soda**
* **White vinegar**
* **Salt**
* **Olive oil**
* **Elbow grease**

BAKING SODA

* Keep an open box of baking soda in the fridge to stave off the smell of overripe produce.

* To reduce garbage odor, sprinkle the bottom of the garbage can with baking soda.

* To clean surfaces, sprinkle baking soda on a damp cloth. Wipe, then rinse with clean water.

* To remove stubborn stains from most surfaces, use a baking soda paste (three parts baking soda to one part water). Apply, let stand until dry, then scrub or wipe clean.

* To clean thrift-store silver, use a paste of three parts baking soda to one part water. Rub the paste onto each item, then rinse with warm water and dry with a soft cloth.

* To remove burnt-on vegetarian lasagna from the bottom of pans, sprinkle with baking soda, then add hot water. Let soak overnight; the dried-on gunk will come off with less scraping.

* To help prevent clogged drains, pour $1/4$ cup baking soda down your drains weekly. Rinse thoroughly with hot water.

* To remove odors from a carpet found while dumpster diving, sprinkle with baking soda. Let stand for at least 15 minutes, then vacuum. Repeat as needed.

WHITE VINEGAR

* Mix equal parts white vinegar and water, and you have a great glass cleaner. It also removes mildew and stains and cleans grout and fireplaces. Vinegar can be used on porcelain, countertops, and tile.

SALT

* Salt can be used as an abrasive agent when cleaning pots and pans.

OLIVE OIL

* Mix equal parts olive oil and white vinegar for use as a furniture polish. (This can make the room a little strong smelling, so, as always, keep incense on hand.)

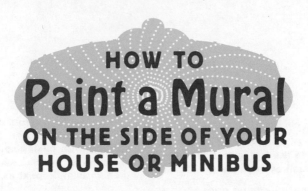

HOW TO
Paint a Mural
ON THE SIDE OF YOUR
HOUSE OR MINIBUS

WHAT YOU NEED

* **A black felt-tip pen**
* **A transparency sheet**
* **An overhead projector, extension cord, and electricity source**
* **A pencil**
* **Acrylic paints in colors of your choosing**
* **Paintbrushes in various sizes**

WITHOUT A COMPUTER

1. Draw the mural image in felt-tip pen directly onto a transparency sheet.

2. Project the image on the house or minibus using the overhead projector.

3. Using a pencil, trace the entire drawing you have projected onto the house or minibus. (A pen may not work as well, because the ink may not flow as steadily while you're holding the pen in a horizontal position.)

4. Turn off the projector.

5. Fill in the pencil outline on your house or minibus with colorful paint.

WITH A COMPUTER (AND A SCANNER AND PRINTER)

1. Use your pen to draw a mural on a piece of white copy paper.

2. Scan the drawing.

3. Print the image on a transparency sheet.

4. Project the image on the house or minibus using the overhead projector, then trace and paint the image as in steps 3 through 5 above.

POSSIBLE SUBJECTS FOR YOUR MURAL

* **Peace doves**
* **Rainbows**
* **Unicorns**
* **Wizards**
* **Sunrises**
* **Sunsets**
* **Blue Meanies**
* **Dancing bears**
* **Purple haze**
* **Psychedelic swirls**
* **An octopus's garden**
* **A scene from *Alice in Wonderland***
* **Constellations**
* **The Earth as viewed from space**
* **The galaxy as viewed from space**
* **MLK, RFK, and JFK**
* **Blissfully content Native Americans**

HOW TO
Pick a Suitable Hippie Job

There was a time when hippies did not need jobs and frolicked freely in the Haight-Ashbury and in soy fields throughout the fertile Midwest. Those times are over. Now many hippies hold down jobs, at least in short bursts for part of the year. Here are some jobs to consider if you need bread to gas up the bus.

- Bike messenger
- Potter
- Musician
- Poet
- 'Zine publisher
- Garden store clerk
- Brewpub operator
- Vegetarian café waiter
- Cookbook writer
- Collage artist
- Bike shop clerk
- Head shop clerk
- Petition signature gatherer

- Functional glass sculpture blower
- Masseuse/masseur
- Jewelry maker
- Anarchist bookstore owner
- Teacher
- Activist
- Social worker
- Filmmaker
- Beekeeper
- "Oregano" farmer
- Ice cream magnate
- Mail sorter

HOW TO
Panhandle

Once you give up all material attachments, you'll soon notice that you don't have any money. Faced with this fiduciary conundrum, some hippies choose to rely on the kindness of strangers.

----

* **Work high-traffic areas.**
* **Keep your distance from other panhandlers.**
* **Work with a pet.**
* **Flash a peace sign.**
* **Make eye contact.**
* **Be polite.**
* **Don't lie.**
* **Look downtrodden but not demented.**
* **Play the banjo or guitar.**
* **Do not drum.**
* **Target men with dates.**
* **Target mothers.**
* **Give half your earnings to charity.**

HOW TO
Organize a Protest

The hippies who were best at organizing protests were the Yippies, the two most famous of whom were Jerry Rubin and Abbie Hoffman. The Yippies nominated a pig named Pegasus as a candidate for president of the United States. They also organized the "raising of the Pentagon" (picture thousands of protesters sitting lotus style around the Pentagon attempting to levitate it), as well as the protest at the 1968 Chicago Democratic Convention, which culminated in the police hitting college kids over the head with their batons while TV crews filmed and the whole world watched. The evening news that night radicalized a lot of people. That's what made the Yippies so effective. They knew how to attract the media.

TIMING

Choose a convenient day and time for your protest so that both protesters and TV news crews can attend. For instance, select a Friday around five o'clock, in time for the late-evening TV news cycle.

PERMITS

You usually don't need a permit to hold a protest on a public sidewalk, as long as you don't block traffic on the sidewalk or on the street. You will need a permit for a street march and should contact City Hall many weeks in advance. If you protest on private property, you will be required to leave if the owner requests it, or face arrest. It is always a good idea to inquire about local and state laws regarding demonstrations, even if you plan on protesting on public property. You need to know the permit requirements, noise limits, specific hours when protests are permitted, and other logistical details.

BE CREATIVE

People can stand around with signs anytime. To get more public attention, make your protest something special. Wear costumes, stage a "die-in," nominate a pig for president, try to levitate the Pentagon—let your imagination run wild.

VERY IMPORTANT PROTESTORS

If possible, get some local celebrities or VIPs (actors, musicians, lefty politicians) to attend. Identify famous folks who might be interested in your cause and contact them via letter or phone a few weeks before your event. Just pick up a magazine and see who shows up to what sort of fundraiser. Woody Harrelson likes hemp. Ed Begley Jr. doesn't like pollution. Martin Sheen doesn't like nukes. Alicia Silverstone likes animals. Celebrities can be especially effective if you can convince them to get arrested. All they can do is say no.

ALERT THE MEDIA

The whole world can't watch if the media aren't there to cover it. Send a press release to your local print, television, and radio media a full week before the protest and call them that morning to remind them. Tell them what the protest is going to be like and how many people you expect to be there. Let them know about any VIPs who will be attending. Offer to supply articulate, knowledgeable spokespeople for them to interview.

GATHER THE TROOPS

Get people there: A few days before the event, put up posters. Alert like-minded organizations and college radio stations. Call all your friends.

(continued)

COMMUNICATE THE PLAN

Once everyone has gathered, make sure all your protesters know what the protest plan is. Are you going to march? Where? What will you do if the police decide to disperse the group? Are you going to "claim turf" **(SEE BELOW)** or disband peaceably? Protests can get out of control quickly if everyone isn't on the same page. Make sure that all of the organizers have walkie-talkies and megaphones.

HOW TO "CLAIM TURF"

Claiming turf is a time-honored hippie protest method. Claiming turf is, quite simply, the act of taking over a location and refusing to leave. Here's how you do it.

1. Move into an area in large numbers.*

2. Link arms.

3. Go limp (it makes it harder for law enforcement officers to move you).

4. Chant, "Hell no, we won't go."

*MAKE SURE YOU HAVE MONEY TO MAKE BAIL

WHAT TO DO IF YOU'RE TEARGASSED

1. If you are gassed, do not panic. Your eyesight will most likely become blurry. Don't compound the problem by running out into traffic. Calmly move to a safer area.

2. Immediately flush the affected area of your body with neutralizer solution (95 percent water and 5 percent baking soda). Do not rub the solution into your skin; this will only cause the tear gas chemicals to sink in deeper. Take a cold shower afterward to rinse off the irritants. Hot showers and baths should be avoided since they open pores and may allow the irritants to penetrate further.

CLASSIC PROTEST CHANTS
(JUST FILL IN THE BLANKS)

*   What do we want? [_____]
    When do we want it? NOW!

*   Hey Hey! Ho Ho! [_____]
    [_____] [_____] has got to go!

*   One, two, three, four, we don't
    want your [_____] war!

CLASSIC PROTEST SONGS

*   "We Shall Overcome"

*   "Give Peace a Chance"

*   "You've Got to Fight for Your
    Right to Party"

HOW TO
Tree Sit

WHAT YOU NEED

* An old-growth tree in danger of being cut down
* A hammer, nails, and two-by-fours to build a tree-sitting platform
* A rope
* A blank journal for writing poetry
* A cellphone
* At least 1 tarp
* A lantern
* A gas stove
* Water
* Matches
* Sunscreen
* A first-aid kit
* A sleeping bag
* Vegetarian snacks
* Containers with snap-tight lids to keep moisture out
* A 5-gallon bucket
* Friends to empty your poop bucket and bring you food

HIPPIE IN TREE

1. Build a tree-sitting platform.

2. Climb the tree.

3. Perch on the tree-sitting platform.

4. Give interviews to the media.

5. Write memoir.

OPTIONAL

* **A Powerbook G4 with DVD player**

* **Audio books and tape player**

* **A Palm Pilot (with Scrabble)**

* **A book of Sunday *New York Times* crosswords**

* **A generator**

HOW TO
Smoke Bananas*
*WITH THE UNDERSTANDING THAT THIS WILL NOT GET YOU HIGH

WHAT YOU NEED

* **5 pounds bananas**
* **Water**
* **Cigarette rolling papers**
* **A whole lot of determination**

- -

1. Peel all your bananas. Eat as many as you can. Give the rest to the dog.

2. Using a sharp knife, scrape off the white pulp lining the inside of the peels.

3. Put all the scrapings in a large pot and fill the pan about one-third with water. Boil for 3 to 4 hours, until the mixture takes on a solid consistency.

4. Preheat the oven to 300°F. Spread the mixture on a cookie sheet. Bake for 20 minutes.

5. Scrape the dried residue off the cookie sheet and put it on a plate. The residue will look a little like burnt sautéed mushrooms.

6. Roll the residue into cigarettes using cigarette rolling papers.

7. Put on "Mellow Yellow" by Donovan.

8. Smoke the cigarettes. You will notice that they taste appalling and burn your throat and lungs a lot, so go easy.

EARPIECE

FAKE BEARD
(CROOKED)

CATNIP

HIPPIE
HANDBOOK

BILLY CLUB

SOCKS WITH
SANDALS

HOW TO
Recognize an Undercover Cop

If you are a hippie who likes to attend outdoor hemp fests, protests, "critical mass" demonstrations, concerts, and various other hippie gatherings, chances are that you will eventually be in the presence of an undercover cop. This undercover cop will probably be there only to ensure that peaceful relations are maintained and won't be trying to bust anyone or bring anyone down. But see if you can spot him, just for fun.

SURE-FIRE GIVEAWAYS

* Is he smoking catnip?
* Is he wearing socks with his sandals even though it's summer?
* Is he carrying a copy of this book?
* Does he have an earpiece?
* Is he chanting slogans a little too loud?
* Is his beard crooked?
* Is he wearing shiny black shoes?
* Does he refer to marijuana as "the devil's weed"?
* Is he carrying a billy club?
* Is he arresting people?

HOW TO GET A COPY
OF YOUR FILE FROM
the FBI

Thanks to the Freedom of Information Act (FOIA), which can be found in Title 5 of the United States Code, section 552, you have the right to request access to federal agency records or information. Does this mean you'll get whatever you request? No! But it can't hurt to ask. Here's how.

1. Write a letter to the Department of Justice (DOJ) at the address listed below, politely requesting that a copy of your FBI file be sent to you forthwith. The DOJ will forward your request to the proper folk at the Bureau.

   > FOIA/PA Mail Referral Unit
   > Justice Management Division
   > U.S. Department of Justice, Room 114 LOC
   > 950 Pennsylvania Avenue NW
   > Washington, D.C. 20530-0001

2. Write "Freedom of Information Act Request" on the front of your envelope and at the beginning of your letter.

3. Include the following statement immediately above the signature on your request letter: "I declare under penalty of perjury that the foregoing is true and correct. Executed on [date]."

4. Wait for your file to come in the mail.

HOW LONG WILL I HAVE TO WAIT?

The FBI is required to respond to a FOIA request within twenty business days, excluding Saturdays, Sundays, and legal holidays. The FBI may take an additional ten business days, but they need to notify you of the delay.

HOW MUCH DOES IT COST?

Unless you are a commercial entity, an educational institution, or a news media outlet, you will be charged for record searches and photocopying. There is no charge for the first two hours of ferreting around or the first one hundred pages of photocopies. G-men charge ten cents per page for photocopies. If the total fee does not exceed a minimum amount, currently $14, the FBI will charge you nothing. You may also include in your polite request letter a specific comment stating the amount that you are willing to pay in fees. If you do not do so, the FBI will assume that you are willing to pay fees only up to $25. If they estimate that the total fees for processing your request will exceed $25, they will notify you in writing of the estimated amount and offer you an opportunity to narrow your request in order to reduce the fees.

WHAT'S ALL THIS BLACK STUFF?

If the FBI does have a file on you, and the FBI does send it to you, chances are that words, passages, or even whole sections will be inked out in order to protect national security.

FOR MORE INFORMATION—AND, THIS BEING THE GOVERNMENT, THERE IS A LOT—GO TO WWW.USDOJ.GOV.

HOW TO
Join the Peace Corps

Working in the Peace Corps is a richly rewarding experience for hippies and provides an instant boost to waning karma.

----

1. Complete the Peace Corps Volunteer Application and Health Status Review forms. This can be done on-line (www.peacecorps.gov), or you can request that a paper packet be sent to you.

2. After your recruiter reviews your application, he or she will ask you to submit three references.

3. About a month after you send in your application, you will be asked to meet with a Peace Corps recruiter for an interview. This can be done in person or over the phone.

4. If the recruiter nominates you, this means that you are accepted pending your health screening.

5. The Peace Corps will send you medical forms; you will need to get a physical and dental exam and then send in the proper paperwork.

6. The Peace Corps also runs a background check and considers your financial obligations. For instance, if you have six kids, they might not think that your going to Africa to dig ditches for no money is such a good idea.

7. The Peace Corps assigns you to a particular country and job, matching the needs of the countries they serve and your qualifications and interests.

8. You will then receive an invitation to accept a specific Peace Corps assignment. Now that you know where you're going, you have ten days to chicken out and go straight to junior college.

9. If you decide to accept the assignment, you will gather with a training group for a predeparture orientation before you kick it overseas.

Serving a stint in the Peace Corps may have been impressive to the other grown-ups, but it wasn't so great for us kids who had to sit through hundreds of hours of post-adventure slide shows. My mother knew a seemingly endless string of long-haired, bespectacled young women who were always just getting back from Africa, Kodak tray in tow. Upon their return, we would all be immediately herded to a nearby home, where a three-hour slide show and lecture on the fine points of ditch digging would ensue.

HOW TO
Run Away to Morocco

Ah, Tangier, beloved by beatniks and hippies alike. Paul and Jane Bowles lived there. So did William Burroughs. Pilgrims included Allen Ginsberg and Jack Kerouac. In the 1960s, you weren't rich and bohemian if you didn't run away to Tangier and live there until your family sent someone to come and get you. It was literary, exotic, and, once you got there, cheap—all the makings of a great hippie destination.

WHAT YOU NEED

* **A copy of *The Sheltering Sky*, by Paul Bowles**

* **A plane ticket to Morocco**

* **A passport**

* **Money to buy rugs, caftans, and jewelry**

1. Purchase your ticket to Morocco.

2. Fly to Morocco.

3. Purchase rugs, caftans, and jewelry and have them shipped back.

4. Groove on it all.

5. Fly home.

ESSENTIAL
Hippie Movies

Billy Jack

Directed by Tom Laughlin (1971)

He's the man who loves peace so much he's willing to fight for it. Yep, it's old B. J. (Tom Laughlin), the half–Native American ex-Green Beret who prevents wild horses from being made into dog food and protects a desert "freedom school" where he and his wife teach kids to be right on and fight The Man. There are sequels where he goes on trial and to Washington, but do not watch them.

Easy Rider

Directed by Dennis Hopper (1969)

Captain America (Peter Fonda) and his pal Billy (Dennis Hopper) fill up their gas tanks and ride out on a cross-country drug-smuggling Mardi Gras–bound motorcycle trip to nowhere. Along the way they meet Jack Nicholson and Phil Spector. My dad saw it again recently and was surprised by how much he laughed. "It wasn't so funny the first time," he said.

The Guru

Directed by James Ivory (1968)

James Ivory has made wonderful, sensitive films about India, but this isn't one of them. Michael York is a British pop star (read: George Harrison) who's come to the subcontinent, girlfriend (Rita Tushingham) in tow, to have his consciousness expanded by a Maharishi.

Head

Directed by Bob Rafelson (1968)

Ah, the Monkees. Opportunistic, shallow pre-fab pop stars, or postmodern precursors of a more sophisticated age? It matters not, as the quartet ambles through a series of plotless, psychedelic, self-aware sketches in their groovy big-screen adventure.

The Last Waltz

Directed by Martin Scorsese (1978)

If the curtain didn't fall on the 1960s with the violence at Altamont, then this farewell concert by The Band could serve as a belated, gentler coda. Rife with guest stars (including Lawrence Ferlinghetti, Joni Mitchell, Bob Dylan, Neil Young, Michael McClure, and Van Morrison) and filmed at San Francisco's historic Winterland, it's a timeless document of hippie-tinged musical Americana.

Medium Cool

Directed by Haskell Wexler (1969)

A cynical TV news cameraman (Robert Forster) becomes involved in the story he's covering in this remarkable docudrama made amid the chaos of Chicago's streets during the 1968 Democratic National Convention. Lefty director Wexler, already under federal scrutiny for his civil rights activism, was questioned by the FBI on suspicion that the production of his film had somehow helped orchestrate the riots.

Monterey Pop

Directed by D. A. Pennebaker (1968)

When square TV shows wouldn't bring counterculture music heroes to the masses, the job fell to motion pictures. Millions of fans caught their first glimpses of Otis Redding, Janis Joplin, Ravi Shankar, and the Jefferson Airplane in this remarkable concert filmed during the Summer of Love.

The Trip

Directed by Roger Corman (1967)

In which a veritable all-star team of male hippie movie stars is assembled. See: Peter Fonda as the uptight ad exec who wants to try LSD, does, and says wow. See: Bruce Dern as the hipster who guides him on his magic carpet ride. See: Dennis Hopper as the dealer. It's even written by Jack Nicholson!

Woodstock

Michael Wadleigh (1970)

As much a record of the astonishing happening as it is of the music played there, this three-hour (almost four in the "director's cut"), Oscar-winning documentary has many a memorable moment, from the Port-A-San man to Hendrix's unforgettable rendition of "The Star-Spangled Banner." Look carefully for fast glimpses of future CEOs.

Yellow Submarine

Directed by George Dunning (1968)

Groovy animation tells how Captain Fred escapes from Pepperland in his color-ful craft after the Blue Meanies take over. Luckily, he bumps into a cartoon version of Ringo Starr, who rounds up the rest of the Beatles and sings the Meanies away.

ESSENTIAL
Hippie Books

Be Here Now

By Ram Dass (1971)

Beneath the trippy cover lies the inspirational story of Dr. Richard Alpert and his journey from Harvard academic to bodhisattva—a must-read for the budding psychedelic cosmonaut.

Blue Highways: A Journey into America

By William Least Heat-Moon (1982)

Driving a van named Ghost Dancing along the backroads (blue highways) of America, Heat-Moon's account of his travels through small, forgotten towns and meetings with offbeat characters is the perfect inspiration to hit the road.

Do It: Scenarios of the Revolution

By Jerry Rubin (1970)

Jerry's activist manifesto will make you forget he ever went corporate.

The Doors of Perception

By Aldous Huxley (1954)

Huxley's vivid account of his mescaline adventures turned on the drug culture (and Jim Morrison).

The Electric Kool-Aid Acid Test

By Tom Wolfe (1967)

Ken Kesey and his Merry Pranksters are immortalized by the coolly detached Wolfe in this nonfiction opus. For another version of some of the same stories, check out Hunter S. Thompson's *Hell's Angels*.

The Green Fairy Book

Edited by Andrew Lang (original 1892, reprint 1965)

Cool fairy tales, trippy illustrations.

The I-Ching, or Book of Changes

Translated by Richard Wilhem and C. F. Baynes (1967)

"One of the first efforts of the human mind to place itself within the universe."

Linda Goodman's Sun Signs: How to Really Know Your Husband, Wife, Lover, Child, Boss, Employee, Yourself through Astrology

By Linda Goodman (1968)

It's all in the title.

The Lord of the Rings

By J. R. R. Tolkien (1955)

"Not all who wander are lost." If you've ever seen that bumper sticker and thought it was from a Grateful Dead song, you were wrong.

The Mists of Avalon

By Marion Zimmer Bradley (1982)

Bradley retold the Arthurian legend from the point of view of the women and launched a thousand Renaissance Fairs. Goddesses? Magic? Velvet capes? What's not to love? But then, my parents didn't name me Gwenhwyfar.

The Moosewood Cookbook

By Mollie Katzen (1977)

Healthy, natural, easy-to-prepare recipes and charming pen-and-ink drawings—this cookbook was a welcome counterculture alternative to *The Joy of Cooking*.

Our Bodies, Ourselves

By the Boston Women's Health Collective (1969)

Providing healthcare information about women for women, this book empowered women to know their bodies, and liberated them from a still male-dominated medical establishment.

The Politics of Ecstasy

By Timothy Leary (1968)

Leary's early psychedelic musings and exploration of human-consciousness issues led some Americans to dub him "the most dangerous man alive."

The Port Huron Statement

By the Students for a Democratic Society (1962)

Passionate, angry, and optimistic, this social and political manifesto captures the rising consciousness of the boomer generation.

The Prophet

By Kahlil Gibran (1923)

Gibran's life view was prescient of the coming counterculture movement, and his book of poetic essays is a hippie philosophy primer.

The Psychedelic Experience

By Ralph Metzner, Timothy Leary, Richard Alpert, et al. (1964)

This LSD-trip manual, based on *The Tibetan Book of the Dead,* is the book that launched a thousand trips.

Siddhartha

By Hermann Hesse (1971)

Buddha was a hippie!

Slouching Towards Bethlehem

By Joan Didion (1968)

Didion established herself as a leading American essayist with this collection examining the dislocation of 1960s society and the breakdown in human communication. The title essay is the best.

Soul on Ice

By Eldridge Cleaver (1968)

One of the most important books in the Black Power movement. Hippies in the 1960s were mostly white and mostly pacifist, but they dug the fiery prose.

Steal This Book

By Abbie Hoffman (1970)

Abbie dishes the how-to's of the radical scene, including how to shoplift, grow marijuana, and prepare for a legal defense.

The Tibetan Book of the Dead

By Karma-Glin-Pa and Padma Sambhava, translated by Robert A. F. Thurman (Uma's dad!) (1994)

This classic scripture of Tibetan Buddhism, traditionally read aloud to the dying, shows death and rebirth as part of a process from which one can attain spiritual liberation. I read this translation to my mom while she was dying. I'm not sure if it helped, but it gave me something to do.

Trout Fishing in America

By Richard Brautigan (1967)

A young man searches for the perfect trout-fishing stream in this weird and lyrical musing that goes nowhere and everywhere.

Turtle Island

By Gary Snyder (1974)

Snyder's poems run the gamut from the intensely personal to the vaguely philosophical to the potently political, but they always remain true to the ideals that prompted him to give this volume the name bestowed on the American continent by its native inhabitants.

Walden

By Henry David Thoreau (1854)

Thoreau's meditation on nature and society resonated with the back-to-the-landers who saw the Transcendentalists as their spiritual mothers and fathers.

The Warren Report

By the Warren Commission (1964)

Did Lee Harvey Oswald act alone? Hippies (and everyone else) wanted to know.

We Are the People Our Parents Warned Us Against

By Nicholas Von Hoffman (1968)

Von Hoffman's classic account of 1960s counterculture explores the Haight-Ashbury and the kids who flocked there.

The Whole Earth Catalog

Edited by Stewart Brand (first published in 1968)

The unofficial handbook of the hippie movement. Pre-Internet, it was a great way to get cool hippie stuff. A new catalog comes out, in great hippie style, every four to six years.

Zen and the Art of Motorcycle Maintenance

By Robert M. Pirsig (1974)

Subtitled "An Inquiry into Values," this autobiographical tale of a father and his eleven-year-old son on a motorcycle trip across the continent is about a lot more than fixing a chopper.

HIPPIE GLOSSARY OF TERMS

Most hippie vernacular has entered the general lexicon, which means that hippies came up with really excellent slang. Here are a few key expressions.

Bag: A subject of interest, as in "That's his new bag."

Babylon: Mainstream society as created by the Capitalist war machine; the "straight" world

Bread: Money

Bummer: A sad state of affairs

Dig: To take pleasure in and/or understand, as in "Can you dig it?" "I can dig it."

Down with: To accept or approve of, as in, "I am down with saving the whales."

(The) Dream: The utopian society that hippies hoped to create

Freak: A dyed-in-the-wool hippie (used as a compliment)

Grass: Marijuana. Also, Acapulco red, Aunt Mary, bammy, bhang, broccoli, bud, Buddha, chiba, dank, doob, dope, endo, four twenty, funk, ganja, green, hay, herb, hydro, indo, jay, kif, Marley, Mary Jane, Maui wowie, nug, pakalolo, pot, reefer, shake, shit, shrub, sinsemilla, skunk, smoke, stuff, tea, wacky tobacky, weed

Groove: To enjoy

-head: One who indulges readily in a subject of interest, as in "pothead," "deadhead," or "phishhead"

(The) Man: The establishment, or any type of authority figure or institution

Old lady: A girlfriend or wife (This expression must never be used, because it is very irritating.)

Rap: To discuss

Split: To take one's leave

Square: Someone who is not a hippie

Trip: An unusual experience

Turn on: To please through the introduction of drugs or some other stimulation

Wasted: The feeling of being burned out

ABOUT THE AUTHOR

Chelsea Cain spent her early childhood on an Iowa hippie commune. She really has milked a goat and made tempeh in her bathtub. She lives in Portland, Oregon.

ABOUT THE ILLUSTRATOR

Lia Miternique is a far-out illustrator who also lives in Portland.